THE TRAVELLE

Wit, sage, raconteur, late Cultural Attaché to the Court of St James; Sir Les Patterson is all these – and many more. Millions of people around the world have enjoyed Sir Les's stage appearances with Dame Edna Everage and men everywhere hope to emulate his raunchy, no-holds-barred life-style. In this book, Sir Les shows you how.

Packed with advice on all the most important features of a man's man's life-style, the topics covered include drinking ('I've got full on everything in the alcoholic alphabet from Advocaat to Zambucca, no worries') and sex (how to keep the wife off the scent – usually using the invaluable Les's Blue Guide to hot-spots around the globe). There is also a section on *The Australian Tongue – How and Where to Use It* which is also a guide to contemporary Oz-speak from Abo to Zipper-Ripper. A large appendage at the back provides jokes for every occasion and Sir Les's all purpose speech is just the ticket for any situation.

The Traveller's Tool

Sir Les Patterson

CORONET BOOKS
Hodder and Stoughton

Copyright © International Services Ltd 1985

First published in Great Britain in 1985 by
Michael O'Mara Books Ltd London

Coronet edition 1986
Designed by Martin Bristow

British Library C.I.P.

Patterson, *Sir* Les
  The traveller's tool.
  Rn: Barry Humphries   I. Title
  828   PN6178.A8

  ISBN 0 340 39676 8

Printed and bound in Great Britain for
Hodder and Stoughton Paperbacks, a
division of Hodder and Stoughton Ltd.,
Mill Road, Dunton Green, Sevenoaks,
Kent (Editorial Office: 47 Bedford
Square, London, WC1B 3DP) by
Cox and Wyman Ltd.,
Cardiff Road, Reading.

Contents

Acknowledgments

Sir Les would like to thank the following people for their help:

Photographers: Ric Gemmell, Mark Bourdillon, Phillip Jackson, Chris Lord and London Weekend Television.

Models: Kelly Jaegger, Gwen, Nikki Critcher and Rachel Boehm.

DEDICATED TO MY OLD MATE
THE AUSTRALIAN TAXPAYER AND EDWARD CLARK,
A BATTLER FROM WAY BACK

Dr. Sir Les Patterson K.C.B.

The Author would like to thank the Australian
Chapter of the International Cheese Board
(Literature Division) whose generous grant
made this book possible.

Introduction

By Professor Brian Malouf,
London Community Centre
for Anglo-Australian Understanding

Now that world attention has shifted to the great sub-Continent of the South Pacific as today's major theatre of events, there is a crying need for a cogent explanation of the potency and importance of Australia. Australia-watchers agree that the thrust and style of this young nation is exemplified in the life and career of one great son of Australia. That man is, of course, Dr Sir Leslie Colin Patterson – career diplomat, wit, sage, raconteur, late Cultural Attaché to the Court of St James, plenipotentiary, fillum producer, and Chairman of the Australian Chapter of the International Cheese Board – adulated by his countrymen as being, for them, Ronald Reagan, the Pope, Prince Philip, Henry Kissinger, Rupert Murdoch, Lee Marvin, Bob Hawke and Pierre Trudeau, to name a few, all rolled into one.

Needless to say, there have been many attempts to get Sir Leslie to wet his nib – even to dictate a memorandum – but until now no-one has met with success. Now a hand-selected team of attractive, yet talented, research assistants have coaxed and wheedled from the great man an alluring and penetrating volume – a *vademecum* and commonplace book *par excellence* that will have pride of place on any Australian's bookshelf whether at home or abroad.

It will be a mandatory manual for those intending to visit

or emigrate to Australia, as well as for those to whom the idea had never occurred; an imperative for every member of the Australian Diplomatic Corps wishing to raise his sights a little; *de rigueur* for the discerning American anxious to acquaint himself with, as he might put it, the spot on the globe 'where the action is' today, and which recent military scholarship now points to as the true victor of the Second World War. Indeed, any professional person with Australia at the top of his itinerary, and who wishes to stick with the winners, will be nowhere without *The Traveller's Tool*.

Australia's most articulate high-flyer lays before the reader in these pages the experience of a lifetime. There is a dictionary of useful words from 'abo' to 'zipper-sniffer', including many basic Australian phrases to help out in any situation – be it at the dry-cleaners's or pharmicist's in Australia, a Royal garden party in down-town London or in the rest-room of an up-market eatery *anywhere* when accosted by an importunate attendant – one is given a stimulating insight into the mind of a typical Australian family man on the move. It will help legal eagles get to the bottom of the endless Royal Commissions now a feature of Austral life and affords the reader a rare glimpse of corruption Down Under through the eyes of a deeply concerned, yet eminently approachable trouble-shooter with a track record equal to none.

There are, however, topics in this book to cause feminists to squirm and anti-discrimation ratbags to squawk ineffectually. For Sir Leslie calls a spade a spade and this is no book for the namby-pamby. The Traveller's Tool is a man's man's manual – an up-to-the-minute treatise on the mores, morals and manners of his beloved, wide-brown continent. Cheek by jowl with the niceties of Australian political and up-market life there is the odd lovable anecdote of a franker nature – the kind that has won him his following at home and abroad as one of Australia's more acceptable and charismatic rough diamonds. *Sex Down*

Under – What a Red-blooded Bloke Might Come Up Against is a self-explanatory chapter title typical of the book's state-of-the-art approach to matters that the majority of readers will have in hand as they fondle the raunchy reading material. Other chapters cover cocktails and hangover cures, the do's and don't's for the professional adulterer and family man, and Les's tips on sartorial matters which will ensure acceptance in every Australian circle.

In a recent press release Sir Leslie writes, 'I only hope my book will be seized on by sociologists, etymologists and sexologists alike and by a swelling world population who recognise that Australia is the funniest country in the cosmos. It will make the ideal present for the occasional person who doesn't realise that Australia is *meant* to be funny, for Australiaphobes or for anyone who doesn't see the point of Australia at all. With my book on your bedside table next to the Nivea the sheilahs will know they're in the hands of a professional and, like any red-blooded Australian male, you'll be able to cry yourself to sleep – be it on your own or someone else's pillow – muttering my own Australian motto: *no worries.*'

B.M. 1985

1

My Tool in Your Hands

I'm a man on the move. I'd reckon that in the last couple of years I've been that mobile I wouldn't have had two shits in the same toilet. My wife, former model, the Lady Gwen Patterson, has got a map of the world on the wall of our ensuite bedroom, and she follows my diplomatic progress with a flag on a toothpick. Needless to say, in recent years that old wall map's had considerably more pricks than Lady Gwen.

I'm an Australian and proud of it, but my diplomatic career has turned me into an international property whether I like it or not. I'm a man's man and I call a spade a spade, so if you're a blue nosed wowser (q.v.), a stuffed shirt, a raving pillow-biter or a loony old lezzo with a face like a half-sucked mango, I'd chuck this book away now, because in the pages that follow, I employ the direct no-holds-barred lingo of a senior Australian diplomat at the top of his profession and the height of his sexual powers. Between you and me I don't reckon this a book for women neither.*

If my old mother perused a copy, she'd most likely shit

* I'd like to direct you ladies' attention to my appendage. It's a long one, but I don't think you'll have any complaints. I tested it on a few literary sheilahs and high-flying feminists, and although they found it a bit of a handful at first, at the end of the day, very few of them reckoned it was too hard to swallow.

herself, though not necessarily because of my fearless disclosures, but because according to the matron at the Ghost Gums Geriatric Facility (VIP wing) mum drops her bundle whenever she feels like it these days, God bless her heart.

Publishers have been putting the hard word on me for yonks to spill the beans, tell it like it is and tip the bucket on my elitist right-wing political sparring-partners, but when you're an international high-flyer like me – a flaming *consultant* for Christ's sake – you gotta be bi-partisan without fear or flavour across the board at the end of the day. Are you with me?

While I was Australian Cultural Attaché to the Court of St James in London, England, I got to suss out the Brits pretty well. I learned what makes a pommy tick, slower than most people admittedly, and I learned amongst other things how to get 15 Englishmen into the back of a VW – make one a trade union executive and the rest of them will crawl up his arse! This kind of knowledge and know-how has been screaming out for publication but in my chock-a-block ongoing scenario, when I've been known to be too busy to phone the wife after one of her hysterectomies, it's a miracle I've dictated thus far. In fact, if you were lying where I am, looking up the leather mini of the spunky little hornbag who's typing this out, I doubt if you'd be in a literary frame of mind either.

Nerida Murphy's her name, from Tasmania, and she is blushing like a beetroot as I drag little personal touches like this into my bestseller. The Secretarial Agency sent her round this morning to do relief work, but she's a good Catholic and so far she hasn't taken off anything more than her ear-rings, which are of the chunky punky variety and a bit of a health hazard if you happen to be down on your knees with a senior Australian public servant holding onto your ears like grim death.

I always get the Secretarial Agency to shoot me round a long line-up of nubile young research assistants and

I generally screen them by taking a squizz through the two-way mirror I've had built into the ladies' powder room of my headquarters at the International Australian Cheese, Fillum and Opera Board at Cheddar House. I generally pick a secretary with a couple of love-bites on her neck because it tells me she's done the dirty deed the night before with some poor bastard in the back seat of a second hand Dolomite and chances are she'll gladly cop a tongue sandwich from a mature smooth-talking man of the world with access to limmo and a pocket full of celluloid.

There's safety in numbers I always say, and some of the best knee-tremblers and one night stands I've ever enjoyed have been with a nice lass who's just announced her engagement. In my book she's always the type who, hours before the priest turns her into a one prick princess, will scream for a no-strings-attached caring relationship on the office floor with a happily married man.

But let's face it, my office is usually a Samsonite briefcase, my wardrobe is a drip-dry powder-blue crimpolene safari suit hanging in the first class locker of a Qantas jumbo and, contrary to the popular romantic image of a roving randy ambassador, my sex life, more often than not, takes place in a Dettol-scented Singapore motel room with a couple of bits of yellow velvet and a cucumber. They're that desperate for the white man's walloper over there that they don't even bother to get your Amex authorised before coming across with the goods. With my strict Mick upbringing I've always drawn the line at bunging a bird on Diner's. (Think that one over.)

Gone are the bad old days when a man had to leave twenty readies beside the washbasin. The old credit card has revolutionised the extramarital root. In this day and age you're unlucky to strike a sheilah who won't accept celluloid, although make sure you pick an escort agency or a rub-and-tug shop with a name like a restaurant in case a nosey spouse casts a curious eye over your counterfoils. My

Gwen, who's as good as gold, bless her heart, once asked me out of the blue if I'd had a tasty mouthful at the Purple Orchid, and I could honestly own up that I had. *With me?* Certainly hair pie was never one of my beloved wife's specialities.

2
What is Australian Style?

A lot of blokes, no doubt trying to brown-nose their way into my good books, reckon I've got style. They used to say I had charisma too, which is an old aboriginal expression boiling down to roughly the same thing. But watch out if the Media call you charismatic. Next year they'll be calling you an arrogant dickhead. Ask any politico if you reckon I'm talking through me bum.

Let's face it though; style comes naturally to Australians. Look at our lifesavers. You can see them any day of the week oiling up their superlative physiques on our world-class beaches. Look at the men and the boys of our Shark Patrol too, on a stinking hot day when the sirens go. Chances are it's a routine death's head jelly-fish scare, or a freak shoal of deadly surf-roaches they've picked up on their highly sensitive off-shore radar. Just maybe, it's a Tasmanian toad fish on heat, who's caught a provocative underwater sniff of some topless sheila with the curse. Unless our boys are on the alert, and ready to blast that randy old toady out of the Pacific, chances are that topless lass could be bottomless in seconds flat.

When a typical Australian Aquatic Pest Patrol goes into action, even Stevie Wonder could see they've got style coming out of their arseholes. Whether they're wiping out an infestation of beach-leech or launching surfboard reprisals against a well-orchestrated horror attack from a bunch of razor-toothed tiger sharks, these crack squads of spunky sun-bronzed vigilantes have made our risk-prone resorts a cynosure for world style-watchers.

To those cynics who say Australian beaches are next to useless in terms of safe swimming, I say a categorical 'bull-shit'. Pig's arse our beaches are dangerous! We've only lost one Prime Minister to sharks in living memory, and *that's debatable*. Some whizz kids have even determined that Harold Holt wasn't sucked off a rock by a Noah. There's a growing body of informed opinion reckons he was picked up by a chink sub and dropped off in East Berlin where Errol Flynn (a Tasmanian screen personality incidentally) is reportedly very much alive and kicking for Christ's sake.

Thanks to our super-stylish shore squads, Aussie beaches are safe for everyone except swimmers and the occasional seventeen-year-old female sun-worshipper who never guessed she had a surprise appointment with fifteen surf studs behind a changing facility. Our stylish lifesavers would head the queue in any gang-bang on the planet. They certainly notch up more than their fair share of bearded clams, although us diplomats and the odd Australian high court judge run them pretty close in the shagging stakes.

But style, Aussie-style isn't just bronzed biceps and a pair of ultra-brief water-repellant elasticised Lycra nut-chokers. Every time my politically improbable mate and old sparring partner, Rupert Murdoch, goes out shopping for a newspaper or a fillum company, he tells the world something pretty pivotal about our way of doing business down under. 'I want what I want when I want it' is our pragfuckinmatic approach to that pathetic old pommie put-off; 'You'll get what you get when you get it'.

In England they've got Valium in the water supply, which is why the place moves about as fast as a snail with piles. The whole pommie economy is based on everyone doing a shithouse job as slowly as possible, so that you or some other no-hoper has to do it all over again, which fills in time and clips a few inches off the dole queue. If a miracle happened and the poms produced a handful of honest, efficient tradesmen who could turn in a good job first time round, the whole country would go down the tubes.

Naturally, the Brits call us Australians 'workaholics' which might surprise anyone visiting an Aussie building site in January or any time of the year after three-thirty in the arvo, but I guess the average Aussie working man can really slog it out when he has to, whether he's bunging a new jacuzzi in his beach house, or locking in an advertising deal over the third Black Forest gâteau and Irish coffee at some dimly lit eatery run by a couple of cordon blue pillow-biters.

Take my wife

They tell me that our womenfolk are world class trend-setters which can only mean they've never bumped into my wife (former model Bambi Dolan) on a Saturday morning when she's squaring off the milkman in the stained old pink chenille brunch coat I gave her the money to buy the last time I was home for Mother's Day. Bless her heart, the famous Bambi Dolan bone structure which had some of Australia's top fashion photographers creaming their Kodaks back in the rock and rolling 40's, is down the tubes.

These days the lady wife spends a good deal of time on her front doorstep one way and another, either staring up the street for a sight of my official limmo on one of its rare appearances on the family horizon, or waiting for the postman to bring back the results of her latest tests. Gwennie, my number one Gofer, has had more explora-tories than I've had overseas fact-finding missions, bless her heart. In fact, you could say she's had more ray treatments than Buck Rogers. Still, let's face it, illness gives a woman an interest and my heart goes out to a lot of my colleagues whose wives are as healthy as buggery, and could easily give them what they'd rather get somewhere else. At the end of the day, we blokes are a pretty old fashioned moralistic lot, and we can only have a bit of harmless extramarital fun with a clear conscience when we know for sure our wives are in hospital, bless their hearts.

Mind you, you ought to see Gwen in a decent dress when the hormone pills are working. She can still look like she did in the talcum powder advertisement she posed for yonks ago that used to be in every tram in Australia. Admittedly, it was only her hands wiping a baby's arse, but those photogenic mitts of hers got her the big job stroking the Whitmont shirt and jerking off a bottle of Rosella tomato sauce into a meat pie.

In her day, Gwennie was the highest paid hand model in Australia – though I always got it on the house. But I guess Gwen's price might have dropped if the lens had travelled north of her wrist, God love her.

A lot of political big-shots I know have traded in their wives lately for younger and more politically expedient hornbags with experience as investigative journalists, fillum producers or airline stewardesses and all that implies in the layover period. But my famous marriage has survived the inevitable stress and strain of a meteoric career. Although let's face it, Gwen's human, and there have probably been times when she's kicked herself for being a good Catholic.

But I'm talking about style and I'm sorry if I get side tracked. It's just that my current research assistant told me this morning that I'd put the dick back into dictation, and right now she's got her feet on the desk, affording me a ring-side view of the map of Tasmania. And if you don't know what that is, it's a thickly wooded triangular appendage in the southern hemisphere with a reputation for mouth-watering seafood. Are you with me?

3

My Homeland

Some Misconceptions

On a recent freebie in the South of France at the Australian taxpayer's expense, I bumped into a Yank delegate who'd never even heard of Australia. 'Turn left at Honolulu' I quietly advised the bastard, thinking to myself he'd probably end up in New Zealand which would serve him fucking well right.

Australia's role in winning the Second World War has been overlooked to buggery by historians. In point of established fact, if we hadn't got off our freckles when we did, when the Yanks were baring their backsides to those slit-eyed yeller nips, there'd be a lot more Jap restaurants in Los Angeles, that's for sure!

Christ knows what this conference in the South of France was all about incidentally. I was probably wearing my cheese hat, or doing my bit for the burgeoning Oz fillum industry at the time, throwing a prawns and lager bash for a bunch of assorted dickheads, journos and fillum distributors who couldn't distribute their own piss in a hurricane. Since the good old days when being an Australian movie mongul was the equivalent of an open cheque and a starlet sandwich every day for breakfast, things have changed somewhat.

Before the unions got too hungry and a few nosey investigators started querying the shonky books, our home-grown Oz fillum producers were on Easy Street,

Fat City. *No worries*. You'd spot our monogrammed, hand-tailored Singapore suits from the Polo Mint lounge in Beverly Hills to the best table in the Carlton Motel, Cannes. Unfortunately, thanks to a few snooping accountants and the odd ten million dollar Oz epic that was so shithouse it never copped a release, the arse has dropped out of the Australian fillum industry.

About the only blokes who clean up now are a few union officials and smooth talking 'advisors' and gurus with their hands in the till and their tongues up the government's brownie. If they weren't all good socialists, I'd smell a rat.

It's a big responsibility fronting for Australia, particularly at international junkets where you can strike an ignorant prick who's never looked at a map of the southern hemisphere or wondered who pinched the Americas fuckin' Cup. But our tourists are really leaving their mark world wide, and this book is for them.

Pooftah's Paradise?

The odd, *and I mean odd*, airline steward and a few of our Yartz Festival co-ordinators have given the world the false impression that Australia is swarming with raving shirt-lifters and pillow-biters. I've even heard Sydney – the home of our superlative lifesavers and taxi-drivers – described in one foreign rag as 'the gay capital of the world' for Christ's sake! Well, all I can say is that I've knocked around the traps and I've lived in Australia man and boy for donkey's years, and in all that time nobody's ever tried to slip their pollywaffle up my doughnut.

Sure we all know it goes on, and as a matter of fact, I've got it on reliable authority that most of our museum directors are demon date-packers. In London and New York they're a pushover when some crafty dealer wants to flog a bit of shonky slow-moving merchandise to an Australian art gallery. When our bloke minces in with his little moustache and lobe stud, all they do is line up a salesman with a donger like a baby's arm who isn't fussy where he puts it. Before he can flash it, our bloke's whipped out his cheque-book and the Australian taxpayer has got another six-figure wanker on the wall. But don't run away with the idea that every Australian you meet likes drilling for vegemite. Visiting pillow-biters have had a few nasty surprises in my homeland, and the casualty departments of some of our big hospitals have seen what can happen to cruising tourists who try putting the hard word on the wrong bloke having a quiet smoke in an all-night dunny.

While I'm on this unsavoury topic, I'd be a mug if I didn't admit that we've got our fair share of lezzos in Australia. During the war, my Auntie Bob was in the Air Force, and once when Uncle Nev got as full as a bull's bum, he told me she'd been *got* at by a pack of 'Daphnes'. After that, she turned peculiar and she never let him get his end in again.

Auntie Bob used to shoot through for long weekends with some of her unmarried bridge-playing cronies, and Uncle Neville reckons it was a *lay down misère* that they were all a bunch of raving muff-munchers.

But let's face it, there's nothing one sheilah can do to another that we can't do better, though if you could see some of the boiler-suited ballbreakers who run our student unions and female yartz workshops, you'd swear they'd all been hit over the head with the ugly stick. With respect, I wouldn't knock one of them off if I was using your dick.

How to Pick a Pooftah – or a Gay Guide to Australia

(Don't say I'm not broad-minded fellas)

1 The first night of the ballet, he's the bastard with the good-looking girl.

2 If a man refers to his 'flat-mate', you can bet your life he drills for vegemite.

3 If you hear a man say something is terribly 'fifties', or if he's got more than one Judy Garland record, he's a grade-A zipper-sniffer.

4 Any bloke who lives in Sydney, who's happily married and walks a dog, who uses the adjectives 'bizarre' and 'stunning' in the same sentence munches the mattress.

5 If a bloke rushes up to your wife or hornbag and kisses her on both cheeks, it's a walk-up start he dances the chocolate cha-cha.

Social roots

Australian social gatherings have been portrayed *ad nauseam* in terms of all the men up one end of the room and all the women up the other. That's just part of a carefully orchestrated shit-slinging campaign that's been going on for yonks. Sure it happens. Even at ultra-sophisticated piss-ups like State Premiers' receptions for visiting Yartz high-flyers, but women like yapping to each other for Christ's sake, and what red-blooded man wants to discuss macramé or tie-dyed T shirts or aboriginal welfare? For that matter, the girls wouldn't deem it a favour if their menfolk started swapping anecdotes in front of them about their last Government sponsored fact-finding seminar in the red light district of Manila.

Personally speaking though, I love women and I can never wait to get in there amongst it. Sure their conversation will usually bore the arse off you in seconds flat, but if you listen long enough, with your eyes open and an expression of simulated concern, I've yet to meet the intelligent young woman who won't give serious consideration to a nightcap back at the Embassy. When properly approached, only a lezzo would knock back the chance of a swig, a cig and a jig with an Australian Elder Statesman.

Aussies are great lovers and don't let the Media tell you any different. A pommie women's magazine (probably run by a bunch of stoney-faced old skirt-lifters) reckoned Australian men never went in for 'foreplay'. That's a dirty lie. I've asked around my political colleagues and peer group, and every bloke I've talked to says he never gives his wife one without first asking if she's awake.

We've copped a lot of stick lately for political corruption. But isn't this progress? Australia's in the big league now. We've got organised crime, racial prejudice, cable TV, AIDS, disabled toilets, and under-age drug abuse, *second to none*. A touch of political corruption here and there is just another harmless symptom of our national maturity. Name another world power where the police aren't as bent as a two-bob watch and the State Premiers aren't on every kick-back in the book.

My home town, Sydney, has always had a bit of a scallywag reputation anyway. It kicked off with a small population of scallywags back in 1788 and it's still got that image, but a senior Australian public servant has got to supplement his superannuation somehow, and if you'd call a bit of a scallywag a crook, you'd call the Pope a Jew.

I hope, during the course of this publication, to explode many other myths and to provide a scholarly rebuttal to shithouse fallacies pertaining to my homeland.

4

The Home Front

The Woman behind me*

*At the time of writing, she's thirteen thousand miles behind me.

As a diplomat and international trouble-shooter, I tend to be all over the place like a mad woman's shit. Perhaps it's a paradox that I am also a deeply home-loving man who is never happier than when he is placing a long distance telephone call to his wife.

I've mentioned Gwen before in this publication and I'll pay homage to her again off and on throughout this book. Tragically, Lady Patterson will never read this deeply moving tribute to her goodself, because she is currently a courageous dyslexia victim bless her heart. She couldn't read the label on a tin of spaghetti as the occasional VIP dinner guest at our home has been too polite to mention. Her affliction will prevent her from perusing this publication, which is probably just as well in the light of some of my fearless revelations.

Every red-blooded man, I don't care how happily married, has a picture in his mind of his ideal woman – and it doesn't always coincide with the flabby old Minister of War snoring away in her half of the fart-sack. I reckon that the type of girl who could really give me a good time would have to be three foot six high with a flat head. Let's face it, when a man's having a bit of harmless fun, he's got to rest his stubble on something for Christ's sake!

But whatever Gwen lacks, she's certainly got some of the

great qualities that have made Australian women famous throughout the planet. As a shag she might score zero, but she's ace at washing, ironing and keeping a man's tucker warm. (In my case she's sometimes had to keep it warm for a fortnight, the Lord be good to her.)

And is she clean! That's a sheilah's number one qualification in my book and there's nothing worse, let's face it, than a woman on the nose when you get down to it. I've struck part-time research assistants who accept lavish expense account lunches without telling you first that they've got the flags out. What a dirty con! Result: a bundle of taxpayers' money blown, and a raunchy arvo on the nest up the spout. Whenever Gwen was red sails in the sunset she always had the courtesy to sleep in the spare room. Currently, they just don't make 'em like Gwen any more.

When we were courting, as it used to be called, Gwenneth Dolan always enjoyed a good movie. Looking back I can see it was probably her dyslexia showing up, because I never saw her put her nose in a book. I never saw her put her nose in anything come to that. I reckon she also knew I wouldn't try anything too gymnastic in the dress circle with a lap-full of Columbine Caramels and a theatre full of couples trying to concentrate on fuckin Dumbo. Was she a Disney freak! Disney and Van Johnson. But Dumbo and Bambi were her favourite flicks and she modelled under the name of 'Bambi' although Dumbo would have suited her better, God love her.

Gwen's listening equipment was always one of her most prominent features and *à propos* and *vis à vis* of this, a colleague who once overheard me tell Gwennie a little white lie about where and who I'd been up the night before, said to me later: 'your wife could hardly believe her ears'. To which I retorted: 'I can hardly believe them either mate, but it's what's holding them apart worries me.' In recent years I've been closely affiliated with the fillum industry and I reckon I first became a fillum buff sitting through *The Song of Bernadette* with Gwen, trying to get a finger in. It's

funny what'll stick in your mind – usually what you can't
stick anywhere else.

Which reminds me of the colleague of mine who only got
a chance to grope his Girl Friday at the Pictures. One
day, half way through my favourite fillum *In Terms of
Endearment* the sheilah complained his ring was hurting
her. 'That's not my ring', said Jeff, 'that's my wristwatch!'
True story, and I guess he's lucky it was waterproof.

Gwen and me tied the knot at Our Lady of Dolours in
one of Sydney's prestige suburbs. The church is now
a community puppet workshop for disabled aboriginal
parents without partners, but on our day of days the pews
were chockers with a mob of my cobbers from New Guinea
days. The bucks night had been a pretty rorty affair and
most of the lads were slipping in and out of the church for
a hair of the dog. When the time came to take our photos
outside, Gwen had trouble cracking a smile when her
bridesmaid Brigit (now a nun) dropped her train in a
billabong of hot, salmon-pink chuck that Stan Blake had
just parked on the top step.

Gwen was never much of a drinker, though her Auntie
Kath who's a nun, really used to nudge the turps, and she
used to regularly piss herself at Confession. Consequently,
Gwennie was always a bit of a wowser whenever I'd been
out on the *La Perouse*. Even if I was as full as three race
trains I'd always try and get undressed in the dark, but
she'd switch on the bedlamp and catch me in the middle of
the old trouser dance every time.

Gwen was always great with the crocodile tears. Whenever
I'd had a few social drinks, she'd always pretend to turn on
the waterworks. 'You promised you'd try and *cut down*
Les,' she'd say. 'I can take it or leave it Gwennie,' I'd
always reassure her. And I can too. Or I could if I wanted
to. But I respect that little woman's feelings, she's the best
kid in the world bar none, so when I'm stuck at home I
never flaunt the booze bottles. Out of consideration for
Lady Patterson's feelings I've got a chilled voddy bottle

floating in the shithouse cistern just under the lid, a bottle of Black Label under the cobwebs in my golf bag, gin in the fuse box, assorted flagons under the house and an emergency flask of brandy wrapped up in my masonic apron on top of the wardrobe, just for the occasional night when I want to stay at home to watch the footie replay.

Home is where the wife is

Political colleagues envy the Darby and Joan relationship which Gwen and I enjoy. Currently, we're a bit of a legend in diplomatic circles, or she is. She's that legendary in fact, that a lot of my peer group don't even believe she exists! And sometimes I have to pinch myself too, especially if I happen to be on a far-flung mission, slipping some spunky little hornbag an internal memorandum.

I always keep a snap of Gwen and the kids in my Samsonite and bung it on the bedside table wherever I go. It's a rare one of Gwen smiling, and a New Zealand hostie once thought it was a photo of my mum. It was neither the time nor the place to set the record straight, and there's been times I've been grateful to that old Polaroid. If you're on the job with a little raver and there's a fair risk you might shoot your bolt too soon, you can't beat the steadying influence of a family photograph.

I've always tried to keep my family out of the limelight. Journos and fillum crews have been trying to get at Gwen and the kids for years, but I've always pissed them off. Craig and Karen's schooldays would have probably been sheer hell if the other kids had known their father was a world famous statesman. Sure, my youngsters are as proud as buggery of me, but I've tried to keep their profiles low and let them grow up like a couple of normal young Australians, instead of like some of the spoiled brats I've struck in the diplomatic community who behave as if they were born with a silver spoon up their arse.

Young Craig, like all brilliant kids, went through a sticky patch when he dropped out of accountancy and then theology, but now he's really wrapped in electrical engineering and computer programming. Although he's been pretty close to his mum due to the exigencies of my top priority job, Craig is a far cry from being a latent turd-burglar, in fact he's now in the same footie team I used to play for and I'm pleased to say he takes the same sized Jockstrap.

Karen's shaping up well too. Facially she's a dead ringer for me, specially around the mouth, and she's done fantastically well second time around in her physio exam at Our Lady of Dolours School for Ridiculously Slow Learners, God bless her heart. And thanks to her speech therapist, you don't notice anything unless she's nervous.

By Christ though, it's a relief to have produced two healthy well-adjusted kids in this day and age, and I'm glad I insisted that they both had a normal no-nonsense upbringing. Once again, all credit to Gwennie. She's really supportive, and a lot of other politicians' wives can vouch for that. When their hubbies are off on extended government business overseas, Gwen's the shoulder they all cry on. She lends them anything they need, from a sympathetic ear or a cup of castor sugar, to a couple of long-life batteries for the lonely grass-widow who likes her pleasures portable. Gwen's one of nature's givers. In fact I sometimes think she'd give away her arsehole and shit through her ribs.

5

So You're Coming Down Under?

The computer has determined that a high percentage of men and women investing in this book are seriously contemplating the Big Trip. They want a book that will tell them what other guide books never mention.

For some years, I held down an enormous encumbency. Australian Cultural Attaché to the Court of St James in London, England. In them days, I had a lot of VIP's seeking my confidential advice about everything from how to go about a business trip to Sydney, to how to organise a flaming Royal Tour. I hope I'm not breaking a Royal confidence, or in breach of protocol when I tell you, in the privacy of this book, that a few of my very good friends at Buck House were shit-scared of going to Australia until I gave them the good oil.

'Thank Christ you're giving me this confidential briefing, Les,' said a young Royal who shall be nameless.

'Until I met you I reckoned the average Australian politician wouldn't know a tram was up him till the bell rang,' or words to that effect. Sometimes my memory is a bit fuzzy the morning after. His Nibs asked me a stack of intelligent and searching questions which probably speak for a lot of commoners too. So I'll reprint them here, with my answers appended. *No worries*.

What to pack

Ermine and heavy jewel-encrusted hats are 'not on' in egalitarian Australia. Rough hewn old pommie working class politicians and union leaders who've sold out to the establishment and brown-nosed their way into the House of Lords would also be well advised to leave their lordly trappings hanging behind the bathroom door on the white plastic stick-on hook.

Informality is the keynote where I come from, though at first nights at the wheelchair-compatible Sydney Opera House cum Multi-Purpose Convention Centre, a nicely-pressed, comparatively spotless powder-blue crimpolene safari suit never goes amiss. Whenever I'm jetting through Honkers, there's a little yellow bastard at the Happy Brothers Tailoring Company in some arcade who runs me up half a dozen powder-blue crimps at a time, and my old mate the Australian Taxpayer picks up the more than reasonable tab, bless him. (This tailor sends me a Christmas card once a year too.)

But don't run away with the idea we never wear a dinner suit. The only risk is at Canberra cocktail parties when some dickhead might mistake you for the drinks waiter. But if you like getting into penguin gear, watch out for the sub-tropical weather, particularly when you are sitting in some prestige Yartz venue listening to Roger Woodward or Dame Joan bawling their skulls off. Up-market music on a hot night can make you sweat like buggery, and you can easily rust up the clips on your bow-tie.

Currently, Australian tailoring, which has taken a few knocks over the years, has now come of age. Most of the suits you see in Sydney and Melbourne are that smart, they look like JR's cast-offs. One of our sartorial innovations is the undulating jacket hem. That is to say, the back of an Australian hand-crafted mohair and terylene suit coat is always shorter than the front by up to 6 inches, affording extra ventilation to the posterior. Coloured shirts with white collars and cuffs are also popular with merchant

bankers and wine-tasters. But if you're wearing a D.J.
a frilly dress-shirt with attached wing collar in mauve
or chartreuse is *de rigeur*. Not too much colour though,
or they'll reckon you've just been to a Maltese wedding.

Don't forget your bathers, or 'swimming togs' as we
call them in Australia. The briefer the better if you've got
a nice bit of hose-pipe to flash. The pommie habit of
wearing woollen socks with sandals has given a lot of our
Brit visitors the reputation for being on the nose, since
Australia's favourite summer footwear is the hygienic
Taiwanese thong (q.v.). If you're an optimist like me, don't
bother to pack a pair of pyjamas.

There are signs clearly posted in most hostelries and
restaurants, indicating the appropriate gear, e.g.

SORRY GENTS, NO THONGS
CLEAN CASUAL ATTIRE PLEASE GENTS
NO JEANS ALLOWED THANKS GENTS
GENTS, PLEASE USE GENTS, THANKS GENTS

Most decent places will lend you a bit of spare gear to
help you fit in with the increasing formality of our
up-market eating venues. You could turn up without a pair
of shoes and a shirt, but most Maitre d's carry a few spare
sets of shirts, ties and thongs on the bottom shelf of the
sweets trolley.

We won't stick it up you
Because they haven't found a cure for AIDS yet, there are
no jabs necessary for Australia. However, rabies shots
aren't a bad idea if you are going anywhere near a Koala
compound, a bandicoot or numbat reserve or an ant
sanctuary. If any of those little bastards get their teeth in
you, you're history in seconds flat. (*See* Kissing Aborigines,
page 179)

Plenty of visitors whinge about our national custom of
squirting plane passengers with insecticide before they

disembark at our award-winning, acclaimed, architect-designed international airports. In the old days a few blokes in shorts and thongs and a fag going used to just walk down the aisle with their dirty great aerosols in their hands, squirting any Pom or Yank they didn't like the look of. But now the hosties or some uniformed vegemite-driller gives everyone a bit of a lecture on how few bugs and creepy crawlies there are in Australia compared with the rest of the world, and how we don't want any more of the little bastards smuggled in by vermin-infested tourists.

At that point, the same team of blokes, only in neat shorts and long white socks, courteously stroll up and down the aisle, pointing their nozzles discreetly at the luggage rack. Once that's over, you don't have much longer to wait before stepping out into the pure Australian sunshine, to be eaten alive by the flies. Looking at some of the shonky passengers I've seen back there in economy, it beats me why our boys don't whip down their nut-chokers and give them a blast in the pills, which let's face it, is where any self-respecting family of unacceptable insect life is going to be living it up and having a ball.

I don't know why my colleagues in Immigration or Hygiene Control don't go the whole hog and get everyone who arrives in Australia to strip off bollock naked and take a pine-o-clean bath while their gear is neatly folded, catalogued and burnt. This would also be a ripper way of expanding the Australian public service.

Hygiene prerequisites

Take a good supply of Frenchies. You can buy them across the counter in Australia, but you never know what might crop up on the plane or at an exotic stop-over in Bangkok or Singapore. Bearing this in mind, chuck in a packet of the rainbow-hued variety. If you strike it lucky with a bit of yellow velvet at a rub-and-tug shop in Manila, the little lass would be tickled pink that you've been thoughtful enough to colour co-ordinate, and with any luck you might even find you've done *yourself* a favour a couple of days later when you don't scream the place down having a piss.

Any members of the gentler sex who have followed me this far should be reminded to whip the batteries out of their vibrators before leaving for Australia, or your toilet bag could ring the bell when you're going through security. You may or may not want every bloke on the plane standing around pissing themselves with laughter while the authorities publicly dismantle your kingsized flesh-pink bush-buzzer.

Always carry a few of the new high-tech **black** rubber frenchies in your diplomatic pouch if you are an old softy like me (and I mean that metaphorically). You never know when you might need to offer intimate condolences to a randy widow.

Customs

When you've got diplomatic immunity like I have, a man can get away with blue murder, let's face it, but here's a foolproof trick, tried and tested in the past by yours truly, if you ever want to try and get a bunch of contraband past the Nothing to Declare counter. It'll only cost you the price of one bottle of Johnny Walker Black Label too. Buy it on the plane duty free, bung it in a paper carrier bag, and when you get off the plane, go straight to the gents and have a leak before you pick up your case to go through Customs. While you're standing where all the big knobs hang out trying to dissolve someone else's cigarette butt, carefully place the carrier bag beside you in a nice big pool of piddle till the paper softens up. Half an hour later, as you stroll whistling through the Green Section with a suitcase of grog, cameras and you name it, you'll see the lads out of the corner of your eye put out their fags and get ready to beckon you over. THEN give your carrier bag a gentle little *shake*. The bottle of Johnny drops straight through the piss-soaked paper bag, hits the deck and explodes. All you do then is start crying. With any luck, the customs bastards will feel that sorry for you, they'll sweep up the broken glass and wave you through with a few grand's worth of duty-free merchandise. Just make sure as you're getting into the taxi no-one spots you laughing like buggery.

If you're anything like me – and something tells me you are – every time you try to smuggle any gear through the Green, you strike a luggage trolley with a dud wheel which keeps veering in the direction of the dickheads in uniform as though drawn by bloody magnetism. Even if you're innocently whistling 'The sheilah from Ipanema', they can sus you're guilty, so here's another Patterson tip:

Word up a bird on the plane, and with any luck, give her a quick knee-trembler in one of the throttling pits. Then, just before you go through customs, on a pre-arranged signal, start having a blue with her. Pick a nice juicy subject like what a shithouse holiday you've had, or what does she mean by rooting the arse off your best mate, and if you can keep up the angry dialogue right down the Customs Hall, you're away and laughing. *No worries.*

It's a psychological certainty that no official is going to put the finger on some poor bastard who's already in the doghouse. Long before I had a diplomatic pouch I discovered this one quite by accident, coming back from a holiday in Bali with my wife Gwen. Because she scorns the occasional medicinal use of alcoholic beverages, she naturally copped a bad dose of the trots from the exotic tucker, and every night she was up and down like a drover's dick. What with that and the frustrating proximity of Balinese beauties screaming for it, I need hardly tell my readers that by the time we hit Sydney airport, we were tearing into each other like a couple of blue-tongued lizards.

Bring money

It's an old saying but true, that whenever you travel take half the clothes and twice the money. At the time of writing the arse has dropped out of the Australian dollar due to

Christ knows what. However, you know as well as I do the economy is up and down like a bride's nightie.

Like most civilised countries in the world we gladly take your celluloid, but currently these days readies are *very acceptable* in Australia. Most of us appreciate cash in the claw, especially if we're collecting unemployment benefit and moonlighting at the same time, which is mostly the case.

But if you are visiting my fantastic homeland with a major business project in mind, requiring official approval at a high level, you'll certainly require a ton of the folding stuff, that's for sure, plus a few brown paper or air-sick bags for the unobtrusive back-hander in plain wrappers. However, most of my more *approachable* political colleagues prefer a nice clean off-shore arrangement in Honkers or Switzerland, and more recently the Irish Republic. Obviously if the project's a biggie like a multi-storey hotel in the heart of Sydney, and you don't want the plans coming in for too much scrutiny from environmental dickheads and local poofter architects who haven't designed anything since they left Uni except someone's kitchen, you'll need to sweeten the appropriate authority with a real bundle.

Just lately there's been a lot of orchestrated shit-slinging at some of our more revered state politicos from a few right-wing muck-raking media mongrels. Dirty orchestrated allegations of back-handers, kickbacks and sugar-bagging have been made. But with the keen sense of justice typical of our island race, we regularly appoint some poor bastard, usually a clapped out Q.C. with a kid on dope, to front up a government enquiry or Royal Commission just so the taxpayer gets the feeling we fuckin' care. Of course, if he gets a bit too keen or conchie and starts fingering any of our blameless leaders, he ends up in deep shit.

Unfortunately, most Australian political leaders are that trusting they're inclined to mingle with the odd crim without even knowing it, with the result that if the crim gets fingered, he's inclined to tip the bucket ungratefully upon an otherwise blameless cobber. This explains why Australia always encounters insuperable difficulties in extraditing big-time villains from foreign parts. Who wants them home anyway, the bastards know where too many bodies are buried.

Gratuitous behaviour

Squaring away City Councillors, Town Planners and Senior Law Enforcement Executives is *business*. Tipping Down Under is something else. Until recently, if you tipped an Australian he'd stick it up your freckle. We're a pretty independent island race and some of us collect a wage packet that big a kangaroo couldn't jump over it if he'd been bitten on the balls by a funnel-web spider. We don't need to supplement our incomes with stingy handouts from patronising tourists. To the average Australian, the words 'keep the change' have always been tantamount to saying 'get fucked'.

But times have changed somewhat. Like America in the olden days, Australia has been flooded with enormous bloody hoardes of ethnic minorities, as if there aren't enough ethnic minorities in Asia for Christ's sake without swamping Australia and upsetting the balance of nature. But being a bit of a radical, left-wing Elder Statesman, I suppose I've got to move with the times and racially speaking, if anyone's going to rock the boat I guess it's got to be Boat People – or *slopies* as we affectionately call our slit-eyed, yellow multi-cultural friends.

Every city has got its little Chinatown, though the way things are going in Australia we'll be lucky if we get a street to ourselves called Aussietown soon, where they will all come swarming on Sundays for the novelty of eating meat pies with a knife and fork! But don't get me wrong, I get on fine with them. My best suits with the hand-stitched lapels and side vents are made by slopie craftsmen who send me a Christmas card once a year, and I just think of them as

Australian dwarves with hepatitis. I haven't got the figures in front of me but there's a good chance they own most of Australia already. They are certainly careful with the moola and they've all got short arms and long pockets, bless their hearts. But running the slopies a close second in their takeover bid for my homeland would have to be my very good friends the Lebanese, Yugos and Greeks.

There's a Tennant Creek behind the wheel of most Australian taxi-cabs and they've got a licence to print money. They work round the clock and go back to some god-forsaken island in the Grecian Ocean at least once a year to dazzle their poverty-stricken aunties and uncles with some of their new found Australian status symbols. Back in Melbourne most of the oil slicks who've been in Oz for a few years would have a swimming pool, a two-car garage and a kid at Law School by now, so they'd have to be making a bit more than it says on the meter, *that's for sure*.

The Yanks wouldn't say 'have a nice day' unless you hit them with half a dollar, but that's because most of them are born desperates – Jewish Eskimos, Sicilian Mexicans, Irish fuckin' Japs. If you were as mixed up as that, wouldn't you be a pan-handler?

I guess in Australia we're all comparatively loaded. We've got a standard of living second to none and we've still got our dignity. The short answer on tipping (in case you think I've forgotten the subject of this informative chapter) is that if you want to chuck your money away, we'll be happy to help you.

6

Sex Down Under

(Or what a red-blooded bloke
might come up against)

Although I am not a regular church goer, I have always felt that there was something Up There, and last night my current Girl Friday (who's a Mick) told me she felt there was definitely something up there too. And there was.

I'm a pretty complex organism. I'm a bit of a mystic, but I'm also flesh and blood for Christ's sake, and although I'll soon be nudging the old three score, I still get that randy sometimes I could root the hair on a barbershop floor. My old mother – the Lord be good to her – used to say: 'where there's hair there's comfort', though I'm still not sure if that wise old Australian saying meant the same to both of us. In fact it meant bugger all to me until I got my first handful, but since then I've never looked back.

I can hear my readers all saying as with one voice, 'for Christ's sake Les, how can a senior Australian Elder Statesman respected throughout the world for his Yartz knowhow and credibility across the board, who is happily married to a once fairly attractive former model with a wonderful family of kids who think the sun shines out of his freckle, knock off the sheilahs like maggots off a chop and get away with it?'

There are no easy answers but let's get it straight upfront. My heart's with Gwen, Karen and Craig wherever my dick might happen to be. I know for a fact most men reading this book will be with me on that one, and if a member of the gentler sex accidentally reads these words, serves her right for wandering out of the kitchen, God bless her. The fact of the matter is that if you are going to Australia on business or pleasure, and you think it's just a land of swimming, sunshine and steaks, you've got a pleasant surprise awaiting you because if you play your cards right, and I mean *credit cards*, your Old Feller could be begging you to get back on that plane and give him a rest after a couple of weeks in the Land of the Golden Doughnut. Let's face it, I'm a Romantic and I'd never deliberately hurt a member of the fairer sex. Well, not after the first time anyway. In fact, I'm that bloody considerate and gentle, I've sometimes paid a high price for it, with a busted jar of vaseline oozing out of my Samsonite.

My intimate equipment happens to be pretty legendary in diplomatic circles but the typing pool would all agree that I am one of nature's gentlemen. On the odd occasion when an awe-struck little Girl Friday cops an eyeful of the Old Patterson pyjama python for the first time, if she reckons she can't handle it, I generally put her at ease by sticking a bit of chewing gum on the tip. Then I quip: 'OK darling, climb aboard and when you start chewing I'll stop pushing.' Believe me, this usually breaks the ice.

The ideal research assistant in my book is married or got a steady boyfriend. If a sheila's unattached, the chances are she'll start crapping on about wanting a 'relationship' just because you've knocked her off a couple of times. Boy oh boy, that word 'relationship' gives me the Joes, especially if it's called a 'caring relationship'. That's a real turnoff. I suppose a caring relationship is when all you ever put in a woman's hand is your pay cheque.

If I've got a relationship with anyone, I'd say it was with the Australian Taxpayer because I've got a huge responsibility representing the greatest fuckin' country in the world overseas. But if I've got a responsibility to my wife, the Lady Patterson, it's the responsibility of never letting her find out where I put it every night. Fair enough? Yet human

nature being the shithouse thing it is, there's always some
stirrer who likes to finger husbands to their wives. You all
know the routine: 'It's because I'm *so fond of you both* that
I feel you ought to know . . .'.

Here's a true life story:
On a routine visit to Dr Proctor, a specialist in Harley
Road, London, just to get a crabs prescription renewed,
I asked him to run the periscope over me. I should have
kept my mouth shut. The stupid bastard reckoned I had
an enlarged liver, blood pressure, a heart murmur and
impacted veruccas. Naturally I told him where to stick his
diagnosis. These blokes don't have the first idea of what it's
like to be an international troubleshooter and strategist,
forced to do a certain amount of judicious round-the-clock
entertaining of foreign dignitaries and women. Sometimes
I work a twenty-four, twenty-five even a *twenty-six hour
day*, but try telling that to a Pom who wouldn't work in an
iron lung! All the same, that quack put the wind up me and
I checked into a health farm I'd heard of, where I had it on
reliable authority there were always a few stray sheilahs
and a certain amount of after hours activity in the passages.

But I've knocked around this planet long enough to
know that nothing is a certainty and I believe in hedging my
beds – *with me?* So I decided that my current research
assistant, Philippa Pappadopolos (an Australian girl with a
Greek father who must have once accidentally lobbed it in
the right hole) needed a little rest cure as well. When I got
to this health farm, they gave me the VIP suite and her
room conveniently adjacent. It was the perfect set-up and I
lost half a stone that week just lying on my back. I'm a
trusting bastard and I didn't know how keen she was getting
until I got a tearful letter from the wife, special delivery
via the diplomatic pouch. Funnily enough I was sitting in
the mixed sauna at the time, having the zits on my back
squeezed by a very spunky little Red Sea Pedestrian
ragtrade lass. She'd come to the health farm to lose about

five stone and talk about food to someone, and I was
kicking myself that I was lumbered with Phil the Greek. I
also had my eye on another horny little weight-watcher in
the yoga class, whose shorts were well worth watching
when she got into the wheelbarrow position.

The gist of Gwen's stiff note (about the only stiff thing
that's passed between us in yonks) was that she'd copped a
poison pen letter from someone. She enclosed a bit of it
too, and Esther, my clammy little companion picked it up
off the sauna floor for me, affording me a very nice glimpse
indeed of south-west Tasmania.

The letter ran as follows:

> Scrubmere Health Farm,
> Little Chafings,
> Near Throttle,
> Hants.

Dear Lady Patterson,
    I am writing this letter to make this as painless as
possible for you. You don't know me, but I feel I know
you and Karen and Craig so well. Leslie even talks about
you in your sleep. There . . . it's out and somehow I
sincerely wanted to break it to you more gently because I
don't want any pain. Where there's love there isn't any
room for pain, are you with me? (as Leslie would say).
By the time you read this, your husband and I will be
having underwater massage. Hell, this isn't easy Gwen –
may I call you Gwen? You see I know what you must
have been through all those years . . . pretending,
pretending, your marriage a mockery. I know you must
have longed to give him the kind of loving he needed, but
it was not within your grasp.
    Believe me Gwen, I swear on the Ching that I never
wanted to get involved with a married man, even if that
marriage was a hollow farce. I fought against it, and so
did Leslie. I begged him to tell you everything yonks,

ages ago to spare you unnecessary pain but he kept putting it off. We even waited till your last lot of tests had come through, but Leslie still stalled, God love him. I think he thought that if you, well if you needed an operation, Fate might solve our problem for us and you'd never need to know. That's so like him isn't it? Then came the telex from Australia. The simple words: *Lady Pat's test negative.* I didn't know whether to laugh or cry. You see, although Leslie and I are lovers, I feel very close to you too. Don't you see? You must see. I guess you feel close to me now too. Dare we meet Gwen? Dare we weep in each other's arms? Weep and then laugh and even fool around a little. I'm young, at the height of my sexual powers, and your life is behind you, a fragrant and resonant memory. Leslie has given us both something very precious and very bizarre and strange and resonant. He has given us each other. Does this sound stupid?

God knows I'm pretty straight. After my lovemaking with Leslie I sometimes think I may be too straight, and I've never been with a woman. Can you believe this? I have never had a homosexual experience! But somehow I know in my blood, in my womb if you like, that we could make music together. Sure I know you're no Katherine Hepburn or Peggy Ashcroft, and anxiety and loneliness have inevitably left their mark upon your face, but when you feel my famished mouth moving down your lean body, my fingers kneading your spent breasts, your wise old head cradled between my knees, my tongue quickening in your navel . . . *Ahhhhg* . . . God, only then . . .

Gwen must have ripped Philippa's letter in half about then because I never read any more, but it was pretty clear I'd shacked up in the health farm with a Grade A ratbag. Mind you, Gwen sounded a bit off her rocker too in her letter and I suppose Phil would have said she was '*over-reacting*'.

The responsibilities of a family man

I've said before in this publication that my wife is as Good as Gold and she's never given me much aggro in all our married life. Sure, she's smelt a rat from time to time. Before I copped the Cultural Attaché job in London, I was doing the five-day crash course in World Culture at Sydney Uni. I'd come home every night and Gwen would run a tape measure down my tie. She used to do it before I pissed off in the morning too, and if it was any longer or shorter at night, she'd know I'd had my gear off at some point during the day. I never twigged to what she was up to at the time – in fact I took her word for it that she was just measuring me for a Father's Day present.

But women are crafty bastards, and a mate of mine, a former High Court Judge going grey, was caught out by his wife when she found some curly ginger hairs in his toothbrush. He reckoned later it was the unluckiest meal of his life because she not only took him and his research assistant to the cleaners but tipped the bucket on him at the umpteenth *Royal Commission on Corruption in the Judiciary* and he had a fortnight inside at a VIP correctional facility on full pay.

What with the steam in the sauna and Gwen's bombshell, I was in a bit of a daze, but I came to feeling Esther's agile green fingernails working over my back. Although I was a senior Australian politician I knew I'd have to think fast and there were no easy answers, to coin a phrase. I decided that my ill-fated Girl Friday's work permit was going to have to run out pretty quickly and I knew just the fixer at the Australian Embassy who could square *that* away. We could shoot her back to the typing pool in Canberra quick smart, and get her seconded to the randiest minister in the business. One thing was for sure, I knew it would be tough giving her the shove and she'd probably hang around like a fart in a phone box until she copped the golden handshake; in which case I knew I could call upon my trusted old mate the Australian Taxpayer, *no worries*.

Meanwhile, a few pals in the security branch could check
out her flat in London and confiscate souvenirs of our
intimacy like X-rated Polaroids, with special instructions to
sniff under her bed for the odd pair of monogrammed
Y-fronts and assorted O/S gossamers.

Luckily Gwen in far-away Sydney never dropped to it
that I'd taken Phil to the health farm and she swallowed my
yarn that I'd been set up hook, line and sinker. Admittedly
the wife had a very minor mental breakdown, but I reassured
her over the phone to pull herself together; after all, mental
breakdowns are all in the mind. Come to think of it, it could
have been post-natal depression creeping up on her
eighteen years late. I phoned her quack and told him to
quadruple her medication; anything to stop her getting on
an aeroplane and checking up on my movements overseas,
God bless her.

Women are a suspicious lot and by and large men are
more trusting. If I ever got a letter from a bloke who
reckoned he'd been giving one to Gwen, I'd have to laugh.
I've said it once and I'll say it again, she's as Good as Gold,
though if she ever did the dirty on me while I was on one of
my mandatory business trips, I'd knock her teeth so far
down her throat, she'd have to put her toothbrush up her
freckle to clean them.

The only other close shave I've ever had was once in
Honkers when an old bag called June Kendall, who used to
play bowls with Gwen, decided to pay me a surprise visit in
my hotel suite. Since that incident I've always made sure
the reception desk never divulge my room number to any
single woman over the age of twenty-five. June was on one
of those all-sheilah tours of the Far East and she'd probably
been boring the arses off the other old boilers by saying she
was a personal friend of the Oz Cultural Attaché to the Far
East as I was in them distant days.

Anyway, up they come to the fourteenth floor of my
Honkers Hostelry – a whole liftload of them with their
twin-sets and Instamatics, and the Chink in the corridor lets

them in without even knocking. I didn't even twig they were in the bedroom until my secretary screamed and dived under the bedclothes and my Eurasian physiotherapist dropped the baby oil. They say two's company and three's a crowd and I might have just got away with it if I'd kept my head down, but the third modest little Malaysian miss in our party snapped her legs together that fast I had to show my face or suffocate. But even though the evidence was under their noses and *under mine as well*, those old tarts wouldn't believe nothing they didn't want to believe and I just told them I was under a Chink osteopath and they bought it. Well, I was. By the time it all got back to Gwen, she reckoned I was brave to undergo the treatment.

7

Body Language

At Home and Abroad

The Gift of Tongues doesn't come to everybody and it was certainly a year or two before it came to me. You're inclined to get a bit lazy in the diplomatic corps because there's always an interpreter hanging about, which saves you the bother of picking up the local lingo. My personal standpoint when I'm representing Australia at a high level overseas is, in a nutshell, if they don't talk English they can go and fuck themselves.

Most travelling businessmen and high-flying trouble-shooters such as my good self and my readers, don't always have a lot of time up their drip-dry gabardine sleeves on a business junket. The average red-blooded male would ideally like to pack his Samsonite and zippered suit-bag, kiss his old lady goodbye and be up to the apricots with a Eurasian air hostess while his wife's saliva is still wet on his cheek – God bless her heart.

Likewise, most international conferences and overseas fact-finding exercises only involve a couple of hours' serious work, so that the remaining days allocated to recreational activities have to be a time of rich fulfilment carefully orchestrated. A rough working knowledge of a sheilah's *body language* can be of great assistance in terms of packing the maximum number of meaningful close encounters into a business trip. No man wants to waste his time and his employer's money on lunches, Singapore Slings, Banana

Daquiris, Brandy Alexanders, not to mention air-fares, adjoining rooms and pricey room service on a Non-Starter. There are definitely a few *no-no's* as well as *yes-yes's* which the experienced, happily-married man should be able to spot even with jet-lag and a hangover.

The Man on the Move reading this book now, be it on the front bench of Parliament, at the hairstylist's, in a disabled restroom or mixed jacuzzi, will be asking this question: 'If I'm in a strange town and I can't talk the language, how am I going to make out with the attractive and available young women I am inevitably going to meet in the workplace, hotel lobby and mixed jacuzzi for Christ's sake?' Fair enough. There are no easy answers but here's one of them. A girl has her own way of letting you know she's screaming for it, which does not require the services of a highly skilled interpreter salaried by my old mate the Australian Tax-payer.

All bodies can tell us something but women's bodies are real *chatterboxes*, and I'm thinking particularly of the young women who pass through my department as fast as a chicken vindaloo passes through a senior citizen. A secretary's expressive tootsie slipping in and out of her shoe under the desk, the way she brushes the cigarette-ash off her impudent and lightly ensheathed fun-bags, her unconscious habit of stroking the sculptured plastic handset on her intercom – all these little clues are her way of telling you what her inexperienced young lips dare not utter.

But let's face it, whatever her nationality, the language most women talk is written on your credit cards. Make sure she eyes them as soon as possible. If I'm propped up at a cocktail bar in Manila for instance, with a nice bit of yellow velvet refilling my Pina Colada, I make sure she sees me cleaning my fingernails with my gold Amex (a gift incidentally from an old pal: the Australian Taxpayer). The sheilahs know a bit about watches these days too, so I ensure a female Prospect gets a good view of my gold Cartier-style underwater quartz digital job with a built-in radio and compact disc player. Although it looks as though it cost a bundle, I pick up a new one duty-free on every business trip as you would be amazed what can disappear from your bedside table in an up-market Philippino hotel, and you would be equally amazed what those tinted escorts can pick up without using their hands. The waterproof watch is a godsend to some of these cunning little clock-teasers.

An unaccompanied girl with a slit up her dress who lights your cigarette with one hand and gropes you under the table with the other, is probably prepared to go even further in the privacy of your suite. If she goes off to the toilet with her girlfriend for more than ten minutes, you can be sure they're swapping stories about how good you're going to be in the cot later on too. But there can be times when body language is hard to read. You might be sitting at a Bangkok dinner table with a sheilah seconded to you by your company's local representatives – in my case the Public Relations and Hospitality Division of the Pan Pacific Ramification of the Australian Cheese Board, and you might have tried all the body language in the book on her too: a lingering look across the Moet bucket, a gallant flick of your Dunhill flip-top lighter when she whips out her mentholated kings after the soup, a polite interest in her longest anecdote, or an accidental finger up her bum. Should our exotic Miss fail to respond to any of these eloquent and truly international signals, then a foolproof way of ascertaining her interest in terms of how the evening might develop is to spill a glass of vino on your fly. Look helpless and let her mop it up with her serviette. If she takes her time you could find a simple way of making her task harder and I'd reckon you'll be in like Flynn within half an hour.

Australian psychologists and sexologists have determined (in a Confidential Report for my eyes only) that if a strange sheilah leans across the table and picks at the food on your plate, especially the cucumber, she's telling you something. If she asks for a third Irish coffee, she's going to want to sleep it off somewhere.

At Home

It is not always easy to ascertain whether a secretary, research assistant or business colleague who speaks the same language is necessarily a mattress actress. Here are a few giveaways from my wealth of bodywatching experience:

- When dictating, leave long pauses (not difficult after lunch) and see what your lass does with her pencil. If she starts nibbling it, no prizes for guessing what she'd rather be doing!
- If she keeps crossing and uncrossing her legs it means she's undecided – help her make up her mind.
- If she takes off her shoes as soon as she comes into the office, it's a cert she'll take off more than that after hours.
- If you can't help noticing that a colleague's not-unattractive research assistant has severe carpet burns on her elbows, you would be well counselled to devise some pretext like dropping your Samsonite to check out the young woman's kneecaps. Should they exhibit similar abrasions, pull rank and have her transferred to your department. It is unlikely that she obtained these superficial injuries from an aesthetic interest in carpet patterns through the ages.

I yield to none in my abhorrence of sexism, but secretarial work, even at a senior executive level in the Commonwealth Government of Australia, can have moments of tedium and it behoves a senior public servant like myself to give the independent, liberated and randy young women who work under me an exciting and meaningful leisure incentive across the board at the end of the day, *are you with me?*

In choosing a Girl Friday whose duties will compel her to accompany you on business trips and fact-finding weekends in up-market motels under an assumed name, you are often required to make a snap decision between a highly qualified lass with good shorthand speeds and an untrained Miss with no knickers on under her black leather mini. In terms of body language, an applicant with the nervous mannerism of occasionally moistening her generous lips with the tip of a lightly-coated smoker's tongue is giving you one of Mother Nature's signals that she has qualifications not necessarily inferred on her *curriculum vitae*.

On the subject of Applicants, you'll find most modern Misses carry them in their handbags in case they get a chance to spend an exciting night away from home. But in order not to get caught short, be advised to carry a spare applicant in the slimy compartment of your sponge bag with the last haul of bath mousse and other freebies nicked from the Shangri-la International.

Point of Interest:
The young lady writing down these words as I speak at the rate of nine words a minute (eh, Bronwyn?) is learning fast, and incidentally she's got a pair of lips on her that could suck-start a Harley Davidson.

Leg-Openers
Contrary to popular belief, spaghetti bolognese is not an aphrodisiac. It does little or nothing to induce a woman of whatever nationality to come across with the goods. I learnt this from bitter experience halfway back to my VIP suite with a trainee research assistant. I might have overdone it as the back of my government car looked like there had been an explosion in a tapeworm factory.

It's a fact of life many women need a little assistance in relaxing, God bless them, and it is the act of a gentleman to help his delightful female companion, whether she be fiancée, Girl Friday or a not-unattractive casual acquaintance secured through a reputable agency, to enjoy the climax of her evening with a comparatively blurred perception of right and wrong. For instance, a happily-married woman or a devout Mick would naturally prefer to remember little or nothing of the lengths she went to the night before to entertain an athletic Australian Diplomat. Furthermore it behoves the man, be he diplomat or drongo, to use every means at his disposal, animal, vegetable or mineral, to see that his partner overcomes her scruples and obeys the ineluctable law of nature by drinking five Irish Coffees, taking off her clothes and jumping onto a water-bed with a bottle of baby oil.

My readers probably do not need to be told that the average wholesome leg-opener does not force a sheilah to perform acts of intimacy against her will; it just makes it easier for her to do what every woman wants to do for a bloke given half the opportunity. If you don't believe me, watch their faces when you tell them something's an aphrodisiac. They can't wait for you to pour it down their throats. Stout and oysters is a famous one but gets a bit pricey, and champagne and caviar is even worse. Grog is usually the best bet because it works fast and saves you the price of a meal; but you've got to know when to cut off the supply. There is nothing worse or more inconsiderate than a girl who parks a tiger in your car just after you've got her nicely topped up and ready for action. The best policy under those circumstances is to lead her quietly to a kerbside bush, give the back seat a quick clean up with her coat and drive off into the night as fast as you can. With any luck you'll never see her again.

Never underestimate the power of the adult video. In my capacity as Chairperson of the Australian Fillum Facility, I have access to X-rated educational material tastefully depicting acts of intimacy between consenting adults and animals. I generally ask a new research assistant to stay back in the viewing theatre with me and take a few notes while I run through a few 'screen tests', though this could equally well be arranged in a well-equipped motel suite. While we are watching the permissive hard-core footage, I laugh and say, 'Christ, isn't pornography boring?', at the same time running a practised hand under her figure-hugging Giorgio Armani blouse. If she says, 'I wonder if the next one's as boring as this one', you stand a good chance of getting the ferret through the furry hoop before she presses the ejector button.

8

Drink

(A few do's and a very few don'ts)

This is a book for men on the move and I don't have to tell you that travelling can be thirsty work. If you fly as much as I do and appreciate fine vintages and matured-in-the-wood spirits like me, you can sometimes fall out of a jumbo as full as a footie final. Unlike some of my colleagues and peer group, booze has never been a problem to me. My only problem is getting enough of it. I used to like a chilled ale when I was a young squib in the public service, but I pretty soon became a top-shelf drinker. Between you and me, I've got full on everything in the alcoholic alphabet from Advocaat to Zambucca, *no worries*.

Incidentally, I wouldn't recommend to anyone a dose of the morning after dry-heaves after a Van der Humm party or a night out on the town with three hookers and a bottle of Parfait Amour. *You puke purple*, I kid you not. Luckily I've always been able to hold my drink and I've never done anything shameful or undignified under the influence of alcohol that I can recall. I've got a fanfuckintastic memory too. For instance, I could tell you everything I did last night in fine detail, right up till half past nine, no probs.

Here are a few useful Patterson pointers on how to find out where you were and what you did the night before if you happen to suffer from mild amnesia due to jet-lag and in-flight hospitality. First thing on waking, ascertain as to

whether you are pyjama-clad or bollock-naked by rolling
the eyes to the left or right. Then determine whether or not
you're on your Pat Malone or whether you've got company. The colour of the company will also give you a rough
idea what part of the world you're in, though I must confess
that I once came to in a Hamburg motel next to a sheilah
who was as black as an Abbo's arsehole which somewhat
upset my mental compass.

If you're undressed, glance at the floor between the bed
and the door and if your strides are inside out on the carpet,
there's a good chance you hit the cot as full as a seaside
shithouse on Bank Holiday. Now, if you can sneak out of
bed without waking your companion or screaming from the
pain in your skull – examine your necktie. More than likely
it's still knotted and hanging over the bedside lamp. The
stains deeply embedded in the fabric should give you some
excellent clues about the hazier aspects of the preceding
evening's activities.

For example:
Quantities of curry could suggest that you and your peer
group may have adjourned to a late-night restaurant and
hastily consumed certain spicy ethnic delicacies.

If the stain on closer examination appears to have been
adulterated with other substances and fluids, then it's
possible you may have 'called'* during the night. Blow
your nose on a Kleenex. If particles of vindaloo or
pizza Neapolitana are present, you may safely infer that
nocturnal chundering has taken place. Now empty the
pockets of your hand-stitched Hong Kong suit. Here, as if
by magic, is an accurate picture of your last night's
activities.

If, however, you do not wake up in your own motel room
but in a strange apartment or the bedroom of an unidenti-
fiable home with your delightful companion of the night

---

* to call: verb. to vomit, as in 'to call Bert on the big white telephone'

before's waif-like infants pulling at the bedclothes asking (hopefully in English) for their breakfast, you would be well advised to dress hastily, vacate the premises and check your pockets in the taxi.

Examine your cheque stubs and if the word 'entertainment' is scrawled on one or two in an unrecognisable handwriting, it's probably yours and almost certainly represents a cheque cashed in a bar or club. Very often in my own particular case I find a few of my cheque stubs totally blank which is not a bad idea if the Head of the War Office is in the habit of stub-snooping. However, your next bank statement could contain a few nasty surprises which I am fortunate enough to be able to pass on to my valued old pal, the Australian Taxpayer.

If, having awoken in unfamiliar surroundings, you have no loose change or paper money on your person at all, it's a *lay down misère* you've been rolled, though I did once wake up in a somewhat down-market Bangkok motel with a roll in my pocket that Carl Lewis couldn't jump over. When I told my VIP limmo driver, a nice little slopie who had luckily been waiting outside this joint all night, he reckoned they must have thought I'd been rolled already.

Look in your side pockets for books of matches. These generally have the names of the clubs where you no doubt spent many hours the previous night: Bottoms Up, Kum-Rite-Inn, The Venus Room; you name it, I've been there.

Sometimes you can't be altogether sure whether or not you've been a bit of a scallywag during the night and let's face it, you might never know. On the other hand the memories could come flooding back in no uncertain terms a couple of days later while you are having a pee or shaking hands with the wife's best friend.

On those rare occasions when I return to the family nest after an arduous global fact-finding mission, I'm usually pretty keyed-up and speedy. Having dumped the old Samsonite in Gwen's front door and given the old battleaxe a peck on the back of the neck, I generally like to hop into the family car and shoot through for a game of cards with some of my old drinking cronies. Although I have a government limmo in perpetuity and a driver, it's a novelty for me to be behind the wheel again, though I'm a man who works hard and plays hard and I rarely remember getting home. A good tip for scallywag drivers like me who enjoy the finer things of life in liquid form, is to wake up in the morning and nip out into the drive just to check out the front bumper for blood and teeth. It's also not a bad idea to see if there isn't a strange sheilah flaked out on the back seat with her scanties around her ankles. Not exactly the sight you'd want your wife to see when she shuffles out to get the milk.

Hairs of the Dog
There is a school of thought which reckons that jet-lag is caused by the consumption of alcoholic beverages in-flight, to which I would respectfully say 'bullshit'. I've worked my bum off for many years on behalf of my homeland (Australia) and I now enjoy first-class travel all over the planet. Wouldn't I be a stupid drongo to forego one of the few privileges of up-front travel, i.e. free booze? Incidentally, I get off an aircraft laughing like buggery having generally lined up one or two hosties for a session later on in my VIP suite.

Teetotallers and wowsers who never loosen up with a few aerial libations generally sneak off alone to the Airport Hotel. They're lucky if they've got the energy to buy *Playboy* and gallop the lizard. Give me jet-lag every time.

Grappling Hooks
Men of the world know that another little drink next morning or an 'eye-opener' as it is known, is the best cure for a hangover. If the morning headache is accompanied by the dry heaves and a touch of the squitters I would

personally recommend the GRAPPLING HOOK, a favourite Australian dawn beverage consisting of a tumbler containing a fifty-fifty mixture of port wine and brandy. When the barmaid puts it on the counter, wait till her back is turned so she doesn't see your hand shaking. Then reach out and surprise the bastard, down it in one and walk briskly to the gents, shut yourself in a cubicle, lean on the wall and breathe deeply through the mouth. You'll sweat a bit but if after two minutes you haven't spewed all over the dunny seat and halfway up the wall, simultaneously shitting razor blades, there's a fair chance you'll be in good shape to order a couple of double Teachers' when you are once more comfortably seated at the bar. Pretend to scan a newspaper and when it stops trembling so that you can read the headlines, you're back in business, *no worries*.

An alternative to the Australian GRAPPLING HOOK is a Dago drop called FERNET BRANCA. It's black and medicinal, made of rare fuckin' herbs. Some pubs don't even stock it but it's so strong that if you spill a drop on the hand-stitched lapel of a powder-blue crimpolene safari suit, no dry cleaner on earth can get it out. It's cunning, baffling and powerful and has to be drunk at high speed. If it touches the sides on the way down, chances are you could flatten the barmaid against the bottles with a high-pressure jet of solid salmon-pink recycled food-derivatives. With your yesterday's lunch in the roots of her hair she'll be glad she had the presence of mind to put a glass dome over the scotch eggs.

In England the Poms fix their hangovers with a bottle of WHITE LABEL WORTHINGTON if they've got the price of one, poor bastards. This beverage has two disadvantages. It has to be poured slowly against the side of the glass, often thus delaying the pleasant moment of consumption by up to thirty seconds. It can also, in some cases, induce slight flatulence which is fair enough if you can trust your freckle. There's nothing worse than casually dropping your lunch at a business function or an extraordinary meeting of the Australian Cheese Board and then having to go out and pay good money for a new suit.

The Krauts like UNDERBERG, a potent little drop known in Australia as CHUNDERBERG. It comes in small bottles tastefully wrapped in brown paper and ideal for the glove box.

9

My Crack-Up

Or Face Down in Hospital

My track record is second to none but most people, including the perusers of this publication, wonder how I do it. 'What makes Les run?' say the blokes and 'How does he keep it up?' say the sheilahs with good reason, because even if I'm shagged out I'm sometimes that randy I could root a rat on a chain (sorry ladies, only kidding). I'm here to tell you that in terms of stamina I'm a human being and currently now you've got a rough idea of the kind of pace I set my peer group and colleagues.

Talking of colleagues, a Senior Australian Public Servant (no names, no pack drill) let's call him Mr Justice Michael Conway of 37, Opera House Road, Kirribilli, Sydney, recently cracked under pressure of work and baseless, carefully-orchestrated allegations by Murdoch's muck-raking mandarins. Mike was a big sipper though I've never seen him drunk and out of control. Well, never out of control. My current Research Assistant at the time said he was a real case for the Betty Ford Foundation and that name rang a bell. I suddenly remembered that last year I spent a long weekend there by mistake at the Australian Taxpayer's expense. It's funny isn't it, when you're working your arse off for a nation of ungrateful bastards you can sometimes have a bit of a memory lapse about places you've been to?

I just made my maiden speech in the United Nations

General Assembly – or so they tell me – and some stupid Yank drongo who'd been assigned to my staff reckoned I needed to get the feet up and the head down for a few days, Christ knows why. I kid you not, I woke up in this up-market joint with a horny little nurse standing by the cot with a fantastic pair of top bollocks nearly bursting out of her uniform. She kicked off by saying, 'Do you realise you've got a big problem? Wouldn't it help to bring it out into the open?' I was trying to figure out how she knew and decided they must have had a bit of strife sliding the meal tray over the bed.

'You can't keep it hidden forever,' this Sheilah kept droning on and I reckon I would have complied with her very reasonable request and been up her like a rat up a rhododendron if her bleeper hadn't gone off and she shot through, probably to put the hard word on some other poor defenceless bastard. She locked the door too and after taking a quick optic at some of the literature on my locker, I realised I'd been doped up and bunged into the Betty Ford Foundation.

Since the B.F.F. is only for pill-heads and Grade A turps-nudgers, I was pretty cheesed off (if my colleagues on the Cheese Board will forgive that somewhat cheesist remark) but I knew from one of Gwen's magazines that it was a pretty star-studded joint and if Liz Taylor caught a glimpse of me she'd reckon I was the re-incarnation of Richard Burton and I'd be in like Flynn, *no worries*.

I'm a Jack Nicholson buff from way back. In fact a lot of women reckon I'm a bit of a Jack Nicholson look-alike. By the same token, one of my favourite fillums is *One Flew Over In Terms of the Cuckoo's Nest* and it all came back to me when I found myself locked up in the B.F.F. Do you remember the bit in the film where that dirty big Abbo rips out the sink and chucks it through the window? Well, I tackled the vanity unit without too much success and in the end I used to amuse myself by standing on a chair and looking through the transom above the door at some of the spunky little starlets checking in for a rest. There was no shortage of them neither, but I'll tell you what, unless you're Jack Nicholson don't try climbing through a transom with a hard-on. It's a mug's game.

To this day I don't know how I got out of that joint but if I could find the nosey dickhead who booked me in, I'd kick his teeth so far down his throat, he'd have to put his toothbrush up his freckle to clean them. I guess you could say I'm old Betty's first drop-out.

10
Stiff Cheddar and Liquid Lore

Currently, I'm a fully paid-up card-carrying Sniffer from way back and I'd crawl half a mile over broken glass to a decent adult Sniffing session, no worries. In case you're unfamiliar with the technical jargon of the International Cheese Board with which I am proud to be affiliated, you won't know that a Sniffing is the official name for cheese-tasting. For this I need a keen sense of smell and because I also enjoy a smoke I generally take the fag out of my mouth when I'm stooping over a particularly ripe chunk of Tasmanian mauve-vein. There's nothing worse than dropping your ash in some poor cheese-growing bastard's show-piece.

If I'm in England I'm also pretty careful getting out of my VIP government limmo and crossing the footpath en route to an up-market Sniffing. You just have to tread in one of the ever-popular Barker's Eggs which litter British pavements and it could throw your sense of smell to buggery. I knew a colleague who gave the first prize for Gorgonzola to an ordinary lump of mouse-trap. Only when he got home did he find the dog-shit on his heel.

I mentioned my nose a couple of minutes ago and in point of fact it is a vital tool of trade. But just because I sport the occasional broken blood vesel in the nasal area, I have been labelled by a few members of the gutter press as a turps-nudger. It's true that from time to time, due to

A typical pair of cuties from the Patterson stable of qualified Research Assistants.

Opposite: Lady Gwen Patterson's favourite study of Sir Les.

Opposite: Kicking-off the World Cheese Congress in downtown Hamburg.

In concert with my backing group the Lesettes at a major London venue.

Get your kicks on Route 66 – are you with me?

Opposite: The hand-stitched lapels took a real bashing
at this Lager and Lamington party in L.A.

Santa Patterson out of his tree with Donna and Blitzen
(two Senior Research Assistants).

pressure of work and jet-lag, I've been known to get as full as a pommie complaint box but I'm here to tell you my high facial coloration runs in the family. Funnily enough, my old dad had exactly the same characteristic and my guess is, by the same token, that young Craig my nipper will one day acquire the hereditary Patterson glow of rude health.

In point of fact I'm as healthy as buggery. I'm that healthy the last time I left a specimen I broke the bottle and I'm generally as busy as Germaine Greer's hairdresser, and he'd *have* to be busy. But what a hypocrite I'd be if I tried to kid you I didn't enjoy the occasional glass. *Never trust a man who doesn't drink* was one of my father's favourite expressions and he died trustworthy too, the Lord love him. I was in the middle of a game of hoppo-bumpo in the backyard under our old peppercorn when a kid ran down from the Harp of Erin to tell mum that dad had passed away peacefully in his sleep halfway between the bar and the gents. He'd never enjoyed a day's illness until then and mum reckoned he was as strong as an ox, particularly with a skinful, and she had a fractured pelvis to prove it.

Fine old cheeses, king size mentholated smokes, rare vintages; you name it, Les Patterson is pretty heavily into the Finer Things of Life. I'm also a Collector but I don't just collect books of matches from the various watering holes I frequent around the world but I take a keen interest too in the national drinks of the fascinating lands I visit thanks to the A.T.P.

11

National Bevvies

Africa – Banana gin. Unfortunately gin has never done my banana a favour.

Australia – Hospital Brandy. I always keep a flask on my person in case of accidents.

China – Mou-Tai Chieu. Made from grain; tastes shit-house.

Denmark – Akvavit. Made of potatoes & caraway seeds 79°.

England – Beer or anything that's easy to make.

France – Chartreuse. I like a green drink. This stuff is made in a monastery. I like something a monk's had a hand in which is probably why I like a drop of Blue Nun from time to time.

Germany – Kirschwasser. The Huns don't drink it; they take a litre and pour it over a large black forest cherry cake, then eat the cake (serves one). If you see a Kraut breaking into a cake shop after midnight, he'd have to be a dead cert alky.

Greece – Ouzo. Introduced into Australia by the Tennant Creeks. Nice with lemonade.

Holland – Bols Parfait Amour. I've never actually drunk this but I often sprinkle a few drops on the Y-fronts before a heavy night on the job.

India – Toddy. Made from palm juice and strong as buggery too. But don't ask how the Indians get their palms juicy.

Ireland – Guinness. Important ingredient in Black Velvet, the well-known leg-opener.

Italy – Grappa ala Ruta. Spag-talk for 'groping for a root'. The bottle's full of old twigs, supposedly herbs.

Japan – Sonchu. Distilled rice wine; twice as strong as Sake, for Christ's Sake.

Mexico – Tequila. Made from cactuses by Mexicans with their pricks removed. There are dead worms in the bottle, but they could, for Christ's sake, be pickled Mexican tools, who knows; who cares.

New Zealand – Kiwi Liqueur. Not made from dead birds or boot polish but from a furry, round fruit covered with short brown stubble. The girls lap it up.

Poland – Passover Slivovitz. 122°. Too many shots of this and you could pass-over forever.

Portugal – Cockburns Port. Pronounced Coh-burns, I'm told by some plummy-voiced Pom who probably asks his wife every night for a Fuh.

Russia – Krepkoya. Strong vodka. 98°.

Scandinavia – Baska Dropper Brannvin. A type of akvavit flavoured with an infusion of woodworm; I kid you not. I guess with woodworm in your drink you'd have to be a closet alky.

Scotland – Drambuie. They say it's made from 60 different whiskies but so far the Patterson palate has only been able to identify 55.

South America – Pisco. A slightly yellow-coloured Brandy; popular in dance halls or pisco-discos.

12

A Nibble Down Under

I'm on top of the world these days but there was a time when I was that unlucky that if a woman got cut in half, I'd get the half that ate. My company certainly makes the sheilahs hungry that's for sure, but unfortunately the thing that most of them want to wrap their laughing gear around is *above* table-level. In my time of course, and after a few Harvey Wallbangers with Tequila Sunrise and Brandy Alexander chasers, I've persuaded quite a few strictly vegetarian lasses to change their habits while crawling under a restaurant table looking for an ear-ring. But most shag-worthy sheilahs kid themselves they need a few romantic preliminaries and so the writer finds himself most lunchtimes briefing or de-briefing some nubile research assistant in an up-market eatery with his old mate the Australian Taxpayer collecting the tab.

Since the Socialist Revolution of the 70's Australians have re-discovered their taste buds. Our newspapers still print the usual feature-length stories on Australia's world leadership in opera, fillums, pomes, macramé, windsurfing and disabled Aboriginal puppet-theatre, but the expanding gourmet columns are shoving world news from its usual paragraph on page seven to the back of the paper. We're restaurant-mad these days and at about twelve noon most Australian executives are that hungry they could eat the crutch off a low-flying emu – *no worries.*

My wonderful mother always saw we got plenty of good, plain Australian tucker and I'm sure that every Sunday she prayed that I'd grow up built like a brick shithouse. (These may not have been the exact words she addressed to Our Lady of Dolours, but *words to that effect*.) These days, funnily enough, I'm not a big eater although sometimes, after a heavy night in the sack or a gruelling fact finding mission, I've been suddenly that hungry I could eat a baby's bum through a cane chair.

Our ethnic minorities whether they be oil slicks, chockos or slopies have certainly given a new dimension to the Australian businessman's lunch. Gastronomically speaking we've come on as fast as shit in the last few years – we even call fish 'seafood' for Christ's sake. Just about every Australian accountant, solicitor and merchant banker with their two-tone cutaway collars and modified Beatles hairdo's has got an interest in a winery and a macadamia farm, and you can spot these blokes any day of the week bullshitting each other over the garlic prawns and red paper serviettes in some thoughtfully recycled colonial-style brasserie. It's a far cry to the early days of my career when the word 'lunch' meant a 'counter lunch' to most Australians – usually a T-bone steak with chips or a scoop, served with a few nice tinned peas, eaten standing up in your favourite rubiddy. On Fridays you could count on a good serve of flake (or shark meat), deep-fried in batter and served with chips or a scoop and tinned peas. Unless my memory plays me false, the quality of some of this simple fare was such that, accompanied by a few pots of your preferred freezing cold amber fluid, you never seemed to notice the aroma of ammonia wafting out of the gents every time a business colleague nicked off in mid T-bone through the swing door for a quick slash or a technicolour yawn. Them days still make my mouth water in point of fact.

Being a conservationist as befits the Yartz Portfolio, I'm into Nostalgia. I reckon it's a pity we couldn't have saved a few of those old Art Deco 'toilet-style' drinking haunts

instead of tarting them up with wall-to-wall carpets, chairs
and deodorisers in the dunnies, and giving them phoney
olden-days names like 'Captain Cook's Hideaway'. Of
course, times have changed and those lovely old colonial-
style bars, all tiles for easy cleaning, are now about as hard
to find as a pork chop in a Synagogue. Now everything's
called a brasserie, with Abba and the Bee Gees coming in
through holes in the ceiling and a slopie sheilah with a nose
stud and a Herpes carrier with a moustache dishing out pâté
and lasagne to the bourbon and coke brigade. I reckon if
you went into one of these joints and asked for a beer and
T-bone, they'd give you the bum's rush.

The majority of restaurants Down Under are run by
ethnic minorities. The Tennant Creeks and to some extent
the Spags cornered the market years ago. Every country
town had a Spot Cafe where they really knew how to shred
lettuce and stain it with beetroot, and you never had to look
far to see where the curly black hairs in your bacon and eggs
came from. Of course, the Chows have been a fact of life
since the gold rush days, and now it's no secret they own
half of Sydney.

I guess you still can't beat a good Chow feed if you've
had a skinful, but at the top of the market we've got plenty
of arty crafty frog-style restaurants who charge like a
wounded bull for a plate of empty pea pods – the kind of
thing your mum used to throw away.

The beauty of Australian tucker is that it's clean. I
generally pick a restaurant that's just been raided by the
Health Authorities. That way you'll be pretty sure a meal
there won't give you a dose of the threepenny bits. The
roaches are that big in some parts of Australia they help
with the washing up. One place we went to in tropical
Brisbane was a dimly-lit joint and when I put my drink
down on a black lacquer coffee table, it fuckin' walked
away!

Judging by what you can find plastered across the
pavement outside any Pub or Wine Bar at closing time,

you'd think Australians subsisted on a diet of pizza and lobster thermidor. It's a funny fact that no matter what you eat it always comes out *à la King*, especially if you washed it down with a few social beverages.

Getting your nose in it

About the best thing you can eat in Australia is the Sydney Rock Oyster, plump and creamy with a grey frill – if you didn't know what they were you could think someone with a lousy cold had used an oyster shell for a spittoon. Compared with the Pom oyster or the Yank variety grown in colder waters which taste as though you're sucking someone else's bathing suit, the Sydney Rock tastes a little bit fishy and a little bit soapy. It's not surprising most blokes eat them with their eyes shut and a faraway look on their eyelids. How you eat a Sydney Rock is optional. As I always tell my young research assistants, you can either chew it or swallow it. But there's one golden rule: sniff the bastard first. Swallow a crook one and you'll spend the next few days on your knees putting a long distance call on the big white telephone. I've seen a bloke in a fish and chip joint (seafood brasserie) park three tigers on adjacent tables before he made it to the shithouse.

Watchpoint:

Oysters Kilpatrick can be a trap because the bacon and Worcestershire sauce masks the tell-tale pong and you'd never know you'd put one down until you felt it coming back up – with reinforcements.

Dark meat

I've read a lot of crap in the glossy brochures they hand out at travel agents and immigration offices throughout the planet about Abbo-style food: kangaroo steaks, wombat cutlets, funnel-web spider soup, quokka paté,* quokka

---

* Quokka: one of Australia's lesser-known lovable marsupials, especially on Rottnest Island, W. Australia, where they breed like buggery.

mokka cake, saltim-quokka Romana, numbat stew, you
name it. Mostly they're recipes invented by a few desperates who always seem to find their way into the Australian
Travel Commission, racking their brains devising marsupial soups and ethnic gimmicks to hook the novelty-crazed
Yank tourist. If outback cuisine is so good, how come there
are no Abbo restaurants in Sydney? It's a pity in a way that
there aren't because you'd never have any trouble getting
a table. You could book an entire Aboriginal Restaurant
for a private function at five minutes' notice and no offence
to our indigenous population either. I yield to none in
my abhorrence of Racism – *and* bandicoot sweetbreads
tartare.

Witchetty grubs, snake meat and numburgers* are also
big news on the outback menu but the average city
restaurant would require a few days' notice before serving
them and not even *my* lunchtime stretches to that. Then
there's Pavlovas and Lamingtons and Iced Vo-vos but like
most men who enjoy a drink, I'm not much on the sweet
muck.

I guess one of Australia's specialities is the prawn, best
eaten on the beach out of a bucket. All you do is pinch off
their heads and rip off the crap-vein down their backs
and you're in business. Takes a while to get out of your
fingernails and for a few days you could kid yourself you'd
had an air hostess sitting on your hand. Talking of which,
one of my favourite occupations in a restaurant is to idly
scratch my nose with a cigarette-free fore-finger and at the
same time inhale deeply. With any luck I can sometimes
even remember her name.

---

* Numburger: A hamburger popular in Perth, W. Australia, made from
the dodgy meat of their local marsupial, the numbat.

13

Patterson's Blue Guide

Everyone's in the business of something these days, have you noticed? I'm in the business of promoting my homeland (Australia). This necessitates a good deal of arduous travel and I've logged more air miles than most kapok-crunching flight stewards. Talking of which, my old buddy the Australian Taxpayer always treats me to a spare first class seat next to mine. It's useful for resting the Samsonite and handy too if you strike a bit of turbulence and a hot little hostie wants to sit down in a hurry on your hand.

Australia's business is my business and in proudly maintaining my nation's credibility wherever I jet, I also try to plan my itinerary around a few of my favourite bolt-holes and watering places. If you're structuring a business trip, this selective guide could put you 'in the business of' having the raunchiest fact-finding exercise of your life. Currently, most of the places mentioned below are hotspots where I am known personally and the words 'Les Patterson sent me' could make all the difference between your getting mugged, rolled and left for dead up an alley, and a skinful of the local brew, a good time, and more pussies than peak period in a pet pound.

AMSTERDAM

In my capacity as Chairperson of the Cheese Board I've structured many a deal in this delightful Dutch conurbation. To see attractive young girls on tandem bicycles with their boyfriends behind them moving quietly up their canals on a summer evening is soothing yet strangely stimulating. Amsterdam is chock-a-block with Art Galleries too and there is no better place for picking up a nice bit of stray. Stand in front of a picture for long enough and with any luck some not unattractive little multi-lingual hippie will sidle up beside you and pretend to be enjoying the view. I won't say that this is an entirely appropriate moment to utter the words 'Les sent me' but a hand-done picture on the wall is a good talking point and one thing leads to another. A smattering of Yartz History can come in handy and if you happen to know the story of old Toulouse going bananas in a cornfield and cutting off his legs and sending them in a jiffy bag to the fuckin' Mona Lisa, you could find yourself in the museum surrounded by a fascinated circle of eager young Dutch art lovers creaming their clogs for you.

If you don't have time for romantic dalliance before the great masterpieces of the world, you might do better seeking a bit of fast action near Dam Square in the Red Light District, so called because it is the red light district. Here you can do a bit of window shopping with a ring-side view through the front windows of some quaint old home-units of available models and receptionistes sitting on leopard skin pouffes screaming for it. Most of the female installations display the full range of acceptable international credit cards for the convenience of the man on the move, and the lasses' tastefully furnished if compact rooms smell reassuringly of Dettol. To their discredit many of these premises are not yet wheelchair compatible.

There are also a few exclusive clubs where happily married international businessmen and trouble shooters queue round the block to watch students tastefully committing acts of intimacy. If you are in the front seat, wear a raincoat should you not be wearing a drip-dry suit.

Watchpoint:
If you're bunging a Dutch tart on celluloid, for Christ's sake chuck the counterfoil in the canal. Not every busy little overworked wife on the prowl through a man's overnight airline bag is overjoyed to discover he's spent something in excess of a month's housekeeping in Amsterdam's exclusive Cockie-Fuckie Klub.

Here's a true story:
A young colleague of mine who's really going to go places in the upper echelons of the Diplomatic Corps – let's call him Neville Thonge, since that's his name – made a side trip to Amsterdam recently on Australian Government business and checked out some of my recommendations. The poor bastard needed something to take his mind off his wife's hysterectomy back in Canberra. Anyway, to cut a long story short, a spunky little student who was saving up to put her disabled mother through university, did the dirty deed with him in a nice clean room with a big mirror on the wall. Imagine his surprise as he was digging into his expense account afterwards, when the sheilah told him in broken Dutch he could have it for free. Nev's always reckoned he was a bit of an ace performer, so he went back to the bar with a smile on his chops and a head the size of a pineapple, but he started to smell a rat when all the blokes at the bar started patting him on the back and trying to buy him a drink. It was only when he saw a big window on the wall above the bar, through which could be glimpsed a young bloke on the job and up to the apricots with the same tart and in what looked like the same room, that he twigged – *it was a two-way mirror!* With the laser-sharp perception of a typical Australian Public Servant, Nev suddenly realised just why he'd had it on the house.

TOKYO

The Nip capital has come as a revelation to many happily
married middle-aged men on a fact-finding trip. The foe that
Australia's superlative fighting men halted on America's
very doorstep are now our valued business partners and
whenever an Australian visits Japan, the smile, hand and
especially the legs of friendship are always outstretched.

I wish I could remember more about the useful conferences, conventions and seminars that I have attended in the
land of the rising cherry blossom, but the local drop called
Sake – which is made from something – is as strong as
buggery and inclined to have an adverse effect on the
memory after the fifteenth toast to Nip-Australian friendship. If you're in the business of doing business with a big
Jap company, they really stack on the hospitality, no probs,
and this involves plenty of yellow velvet in the form of
Geisha girls. It's mind-boggling to the average Samsonite-
basher from England, the States or Down Under, to learn
that there is a sacred and traditional sect of sheilahs
dedicated to bringing a smile to a man's lips. When a
Geisha girl or two climbs aboard, old hostilities are
forgotten, though I'd be a liar if I said that all hard feelings
disappeared – on the contrary.

One of the best places I know to get over jet-lag is a
Japanese bath house. A discreet member of the Embassy
staff or a sophisticated fellow executive who knows the
ropes should put you onto the right place, otherwise just
ask the hotel concierge to tip you the wink, bearing in mind
that it's not always easy to tell when a Jap's winking – *with
me?*

Once you're in the door these gorgeous little dollies help
you get all your gear off, sponge you down and no doubt
simultaneously check you out for crabs, herpes and veruccas
and other occupational hazards of the international diplomat's arduous lifestyle.

Then you slip into a Japanese-style kimono – the sort of

thing you would have bought your wife years ago if your weren't married to her – a pair of slippers or thongs and you go walkabout for a bit.

If my old mate the Australian Taxpayer is footing the bill and you're in a really pricey establishment, ask for the Works. Scantily-clad Geisha sheilahs whisk you into a private jacuzzi and what they get up to in there beats the good times you had in the olden days with a plastic duck, *that's for sure.*

Sexual abuse in the workplace – a buyer's guide

I yield to none in my abhorrence of sexual discrimination in the workplace and there are even times when I let women walk all over me, especially in an up-market Tokyo bath house. A man lies flat on his face and those little yellow dolls go walkabout on your arse. It hurts like buggery at first but if you're still alive after the cold plunge and a little snooze in a cardboard cubicle, you come out of these joints ready for anything.

There's only one Japanese expression you need to be able to speak fluently if you are planning useful meetings in this part of the planet: *moto chiisaku shite Kudasai* which roughly translated means: 'Could I have the full massage please?' If you don't get that magical little adjective 'full' right you might get taken to the cleaners and not much more.

Stop me if you've heard this one:
An old mate of mine who's a senior motor cycle executive, was attending the annual Yamaha convention in Tokyo. After enjoying large quantities of rich Japanese tucker with Sake chasers, the poor bastard found to his embarrassment that he couldn't stop farting, and each fart made the unmistakable sound 'Honda'.

Eventually he went to the hotel quack and explained the problem.

'No worries', said the Nip doctor, 'I fix – open mouth wide please'.

Puzzled, my mate opened his gob.

'Ah so', said the quack, 'tooth must come out', and he grabbed his big pincers.

The executive started struggling and saying that no way did he want his tooth pulled out, but the doctor had him in a vice-like judo grip, and he pulled the tooth out in a jiffy.

Holding it up to the light he said, 'See – big abscess. In Japan everyone know that Abscess make the Fart go Honda!'

You could tell that one anywhere.

L.A.

I played a modest role in a sequence of events that led to the Australian Film Renaissance, so L.A. is an open town to me.

I slip into a nice hand-stitched, powder-blue gaberdine bag of fruit and merge with the raunchy, laid-back, funky, spaced-out pragfuckinmatic throng that is Rodeo Drive on any Saturday arvo in the week. Peter Allen, Olivia Newton-John, Helen Reddy, Rod Taylor, Errol Flynn Junior, Merle Oberon II, you name them they're all Australians who have hit the jackpot in tinseltown and they're laughing all the way to their tax havens.

I played an ultra-modest role in a sequence of events that led to most of the above-mentioned stars cracking it for big bikkies in Easy Street, Fat City, and I generally throw a vegemite, Lamington and lager reception at the Wiltshire Hills Hotel on behalf of my old friend and benefactor, the Australian Taxpayer.

The stars who have enhanced Australia's global credibility are generally too busy coining it to turn up at these P.R. exercises, but with the help of a few Qantas hosties on layover, my goodself, my staff and their next door neighbours, we generally have a ball and stuff public relations.

The coffee shops of the more up-market hotels in the Beverly Hills area are a very good place for pulling the odd stray starlet, particularly if you happen to be wearing on your hand-stitched powder-blue crimpolene lapel the badge of the Australian Fillum Corporation, depicting as it does in hand-crafted bronzex a kangaroo with a reel of fillum stuck up its blurter. To be perfectly honest with you, this badge does not immediately turn you into a desirable sex object and the young hornbag across the bar, tucking into her sunny-side-up with hash browns on the side is not going to automatically open the gates of paradise to you after breakfast unless she knows you are a bona fide movie mogul from Down Under with unlimited clout and financial resources. So flash your badge and once she clocks it, open your Samsonite and whip out something that looks like a script. Chances are it won't be long before she's stark naked and at your disposal in your luxury suite and you've promised her the lead in the next multi-million dollar Australian mini-series.

NEW YORK

An old mate of mine and senior member of the Australian
Judiciary, turf identity, tireless social worker, concerned
ecologist, devoted family man and devout R.C. once had a
nasty experience in a New York rub-and-tug shop. He
died.

Funnily enough, I was in the Big Apple at the time doing
a major Australian promotion. I was trying to get the New
York media and paperazzi to come to my lager and
Vegemite party in the Qantas basement to watch a shit-
scared wallaby man-handled by last year's Miss Tasmania
in a G-string. We were launching an exhibition of orange
macramé wall-hangings made by the mouths of disabled
Aboriginal lesbian parents without partners as part of
Australian Culture Week. Christ, and was *that* the best
kept secret in the U.S.A!

Anyway, the red phone rings in my V.I.P. suite over-
looking Manhattan harbour at half-past three in the
morning. I have to reach across a pile of old take-away
containers full of cold chile con carne and half-eaten chips
and 100 pounds of stark-naked black velvet snoring her
afro head off, to pick up the receiver. It's the Law telling
me poor old Brendan's croaked on the job. I never got
dressed as fast in my life before, which took some doing
considering I had to prize open Dixies's fingers to get out of
bed and then dig for my shorts at the bottom of the cot.
Luckily I was still wearing my shirt and Australia Cup
Commerative tie in hand-crafted Taiwanese polyester.

When I got to the Precinct, Kojak wasn't there to meet
me sucking his lollipop, but a bunch of ugly New York cops
who looked as though their silence might cost the Australian taxpayer dearly. Luckily I'd brought along a pocketful
of complementary tickets to a private screening of our
acclaimed documentary *The Australian Cheese Story* just to
sweeten the odd Yank detective who might feel like
reporting this unfortunate incident to Rupert Murdoch.

You see, I had the funny gut feeling that if Teresa, Mary-Rose, Damien, Xavier, Maureen, Bridget and Francis picked up the *Sydney Morning Herald* one day and saw a photo of their beloved husband and father, Brendan, being carried out of a grotty 42nd Street knock shop in a plastic bag, it could adversely affect their advanced accountancy studies or even jeopardize their futures in the Taxation Department.

Diplomatic discretion forbids me to divulge how we squared it away with the police and the young ladies involved, one of whom was actually giving Bren the kiss of life when he jumped the twig. I guess he might even have made it too if she'd been giving it to him on his mouth. All I can reveal is that Australia's international credibility nearly took a nose-dive and I was up all night on the blower to the Prime Minister and bloody grateful too that the same thing hasn't happened to me. Bren's trouble was he was *out of practice* but I keep in regular training, *no worries*, and I never let myself get too excited. Furthermore I choose my delightful female companions, Girl Fridays and Research Assistants carefully and with a preference for health freaks. For instance, Bronwyn, who's writing these words as I speak, is a former psychiatric nurse and a strict vegetarian. In fact she's had more meat up her than down her!

Watchpoints:

Most Americans don't know they're alive until they've stuck needles in their bum and shoved spoonfuls of icing sugar up their nostrils. This type of thing is particularly sickening to clean-living Australians like me, who believe in the sanctity of the human body and I yield to none in my detestation of mood-changing substances.

In New York and other Yank high-rise conurbations, they'll do anything for fuckin' drugs. The poor bastards would steal the saddle off a nightmare, so watch your wallet. A good tip is to wear a money belt like I do, made of hand-crafted kangaroo hide (humanely culled) with a

zippered pouch. In it I keep my diplomatic passport, my
credit cards, hygiene prerequisites and government slush
fund and it sits nicely under my tummy, just above my
equipment like a marsupial. I've never taken it off, not
even for a mixed jacuzzi and it's even become a bit of a
talking point with the odd female companion whom I have
lured into my suite by asking her if she'd like to see my
pouch.

Finding it

You don't have to go much farther than the lobby of an
upmarket hotel in New York City if you need to dip the
wick in a hurry. Pretty well any sheilah standing around
looking as though she's waiting for someone is waiting for
you, and Room Service is also pretty versatile in the States.
Even visiting pillow-biters and performers on the pink
oboe get special treatment in New York and I know for a
fact there's a swanky nouveau-deco style colonial pub in
Greenwich Village, popular with Australian Art Gallery
purchasing officers, choreographers and Yartz Festival
Directors, which gives every guest on departure a free
dressing gown and a blood test.

HAMBURG

Let's face it, there are a few things you can't ask your wife to do, and one of them is mud-wrestling. Being an avid football fan, I've seen blokes rolling around in the mud and wondered why the female spectators squealed their skulls off with delight. Only comparatively recently in the course of my official duties abroad have I seen attractive clean-limbed young women rolling around in the muck and found it was a bit of a turn on myself. When I say 'clean-limbed', I employ a figure of speech because in point of fact they were *filthy-limbed* and a bloke next to me reckoned they were a pair of dirty lezzos. Personally I think that was an uncalled-for chauvinistic bloody thing to say. Dirty they were, but 'lezzo' is coming it a bit strong because in my book no sheila deserves to be called a lezzo unless she gives you the brush-off or the knock-back.

I believe in giving everyone the benefit of the doubt and there's no better place on the planet for this than the delightful German dockside conurbation of Hamburg. Social anthropologists, investigative journalists, fellow diplomats or plain tourists will all be interested to know that this is the world capital for female mud-wrestling as we know it, or as you've never seen it before. The problem, as always, is inventing a good reason for going there, and you can't beat an International Cheese Congress. As I told the Overseas Conference Organising Secretary soon after I had discovered Hamburg's pulsating dockside amenities: 'If we're ever going to put Australia's superlative cheese technology on the global map, Hamburg is the place to do it!'

To cut a long story short, I conned them into having the next World Cheese Congress there, and somehow it appeared perfectly natural to go straight from a Camembert-sniffing conference to a dimly-lit club where a couple of Kraut sheilahs seemed to be doing roughly the same thing. The highlight for me was when two of their mates did the mud-wrestling routine and you could see they thoroughly enjoyed it too, squelching around with compost in the crevices and mulch up their gulches.

I yield to none in my abhorrence of sexual discrimination in the workplace but, funnily enough, international conferences are invariably stag affairs. It's surprising how few ladies, God love them, sit on the Australian Cheese, Fillum, Opera and Disabled Puppet Boards for instance, but I guess someone's got to stay home and cook tea. That being so, I was amazed to see one solitary sheilah aboard the chartered jumbo taking our delegation to Hamburg for last year's Cheese Week.

She turned out ot be one of the delegate's wives. Let's call him Ian Balderstone, probably one of Australia's foremost authorities on secondary fermentation in Tasmanian Gorgonzola. I remembered he'd married a Kraut hostie a few years ago. It stuck in my mind because he copped a massive coronary three days later. I guess Renate Balderstone must have nagged the poor bastard into letting her tag along so she could look up some of her German relations on the trip. I used to feel a bit sorry for poor old Ian, eating sauerkraut with the in-laws and getting an early night with Rennie while we were all out on the town as full as a fairy's phone book and watching a high class rubber and bondage floorshow at four o'clock in the morning.

Anyway, one night we got the poor bastard off the hook by telling his old lady he had to front up at a major seminar on Stilton at the Hilton. No sooner had we sprung him than we were all down the Reeperbahn in the St Pauli area and sniffing around the Palais d'Amour and the Whiplash Klub. Poor old Ian got himself nicely oiled and the last time we saw him he was being dragged off by a horny little *fräulein* called Helga in a pair of crotchless panties who'd been doing the cucumber rumba a few minutes before.

Ian never showed up next morning and when we saw him

later he looked as though he'd seen a ghost, poor bastard. He reckoned he couldn't remember much about the night before but his wife had invited her sister's family over to the hotel for lunch that day. He was still getting over his hangover – his mouth tasted like the bottom of a baby's pram and his donger felt as though it had been for a spin in a waste disposal. After a couple of belts of Hoffmeister, Renate came into focus just as she was introducing her little niece, the family's pride and joy, the prim dental nurse he'd heard so much about – you've guessed it – *Helga!* Ian reckoned that he nearly crapped himself realising that the night before, he'd had relations with his *relation*, but she was as cool as a cucumber which wasn't too surprising when you come to think of it. Ian said she might have been a qualified dental nurse but she certainly would have failed the practical in oral hygiene.

This is a true story and out of concern for those involved I have changed the names Helga and Renate to save heartache and embarrassment.

Getting the kinks out
The fact is, Hamburg is your town if you're after a kinky time, which explains why my fellow Australians are rarely to be seen there. As a nation we're as randy as they come but we like it comparatively plain and simple. However, and here's another true story, a colleague of mine with a pretty senior government job and a beautiful little wife (I say 'little' advisedly – she's a dwarf with anorexia) used to patronise a certain establishment in Sydney called *The Tender Touch* whenever he was feeling a bit 'toey' (an Australian horse-racing expression meaning restless). By coincidence a not unattractive young lass who worked at *The Tender Touch* part-time was helping me out recently with a bit of after-hours shorthand, and Jacqui told me that when she first met Niall (in a professional capacity) he intimated he felt like a really kinky session.

'No worries', said Jacqui. 'I'll be in anything.'

Anyway, once she'd got her gear off, he put on a raunchy record and told her to stick her head under the rug.

'Ten out of ten for originality', she thought, doing as he suggested, but after a while under the mat, bugger all had happened.

'What's on the go?' she yelled. 'Can I come out now?'

Old Niall was just sitting there on the bed, starkers, smiling like a cat that's licked the cream.

'You'd have to be a bit of a droob, wouldn't you?' said Jacqui. 'I've been bending over with my head under the carpet for at least ten minutes and you haven't even cracked a fat! You've bloody done *nothing!*'

'No worries darling', replied the senior Australian Public Servant smiling enigmatically, 'Five minutes ago I had a shit in your handbag'.

HONG KONG or HONKERS

One way and another most of us are in the business of doing a bit of business in Honkers, even if we're just sitting around in tailors' shops being measured up for half a dozen powder-blue crimps with side-vents and hand-stitched lapels. The Poms still rule the roost in Honkers, slaving their guts out for a few years as merchant bankers, accountants and tax whiz-kids so they can make a bundle and go back to England and drive a BMW around Sunningdale.

Their wives, most of whom used to be scrubbers round Fulham and Chelsea, doing a Sotheby's course, are all called Camilla. They wear identical Cartier watches and they sit around the Mandarin and Regent Hotels bored shitless. In the school holidays or whenever they get half a chance while hubby is still in his air-conditioned office chasing a dollar, they streak across to the South of France and shag the first poor bastard they meet on the beach.

On my innumerable business trips I've bumped into plenty of these randy Brit sheilahs and I could have hit the odd one between the legs like a plate of porridge too, but I've never scored with one. I reckon I'm probably a bit too big-league and such is the delicate social equilibrium that is upper-echelon Honkers, you can't be too careful whose wife you're knocking off. You might rock the boat or, in this case, the Jardine Matheson Junk.

One of my favourite watering holes in Honkers is the Bottoms Up Club, Kowloon, run by my old mate Pat, who's the best kid in the world. It's classy, intimate and stimulating and the words 'Les sent me' will be enough to stiffen the barmaid's nipples, *no worries*. Wanchai is the Fun Neighbourhood and cruising around there at about three o'clock in the morning in a Commonwealth of Australia limmo with a knowledgeable Chow driver is a sheer delight. Rag Trade readers will know what I am talking about when I say that in Wanchai you have a chance to inspect a whole *swatch* of yellow velvet. I like that word *swatch* incidentally and it rhymes so nicely with one or two other words which I never cease to enjoy rolling my tongue around – *with me*?

Chinese sheilahs liking it sideways has copped a lot of publicity over the decades, but I'm here to tell you it's a bit of a myth. The most popular sexual position in Honkers is doggie-style because it's the best way for two people to watch television and they get all the best Pom, Yank and Australian mini-series over there, not to mention the occasional adult video.

Note
Many of the raunchiest bars and clubs mentioned in this guide are private and require evidence of membership. However, if you're wearing a decent Australian-made suit and not just a dirty old pair of shorts and a singlet like you might wear to the office back home, they'll generally join you up on the spot, *no problem*.

Always carry *The Traveller's Tool* in your hand. At the first sign of any trouble or aggro arising as a result of language difficulties, mild intoxication, jet-lag, bilious attacks whilst still at the table or in the company of a hostess, or financial misunderstandings, show this book to the management or the nearest bouncer and say: 'I'm a mate of Les's'. You will be amazed at the impact this simple gesture will have upon your temporarily disaffected hosts.

TASMANIA

Tasmania is a densely wooded triangular island off the south coast of Australia, similar in shape and texture to the Gates of Paradise or to be more precise, as behoves a hard-nosed political trouble shooter, the macramé curtain *in front of* the Gates of Paradise.

The small population of Tazzie has traditionally obliged the locals when feeling a bit raunchy (not to put too fine a point on it) to shag their immediate intimates and to take the old epithet 'Brotherly Love' a bit too literally. It's no wonder most of the population look alike and you don't have to stand on a street corner in Hobart for long to see the odd weirdo limping past who pretty obviously slipped past the wicket when he was born.

Not long ago I went down to Tasmania (and I mean that literally) and my very good mate the Australian Taxpayer insisted that I stayed in one of their fantastic new wheel-chair-compatible high-rise casinos that are shooting up all over Tazzie with their innovative and humane policies of non-discrimination and equal opportunities for raving idiots. As usually happens ten seconds after I check into a hotel suite, raid the mini-bar and peel the sanitised strip off the dunny seat prior to choking a long postponed darkie, I felt in the mood for a bit of dictation. In no time a very nice little private secretary called Meredith, who had forgotten her pad, was taking off her shoes in my suite. In point of fact she'd forgotten her pad in more ways than one and although I yield to none in my abhorrence of sexual discrimination, when I make a deposit I don't like to find myself in the red. *Are you with me?*

This tart said not to worry. Her sister and her mother were downstairs at the bar and for the price of a couple of Baileys and Coke with Brandy Alexander and Ouzo chasers, they'd stack on a gleesome threesome. Naturally I was sickened by the suggestion and within half an hour so were they.

If I had known what a mess those incestuous Tasmanian piss-pots were going to make all over the shag pile, I reckon I would have done better to have just chucked a towel on the bed, donned my Taz-Air slumbershades and knocked off Meredith, red sails in the sunset and all. Anyway, I guess it was only when the bedroom door opened and the grandmother came in slipping out of her surgical stockings, that I did a fast bunk. I've nothing against grandmothers but I figured that if things proceeded the way they were going, old grandpa would be arriving at any tick of the clock for his piece of the action.

Currently, while on the subject of the Map of Tasmania, a mate of mine bought a blonde wig for his wife but when he called into the salon to pick it up, he asked the sheilah behind the counter if she'd wrap it up so he wouldn't have to carry it home on the train in front of the people. 'No worries', she said.

While she was wrapping it up he took an optic around the shop and noticed a rack of small circular rings of hair. When he asked the girl what they were she told him they were called 'Pussy Wigs' or 'Merkins' to use an old English Aboriginal expression. Apparently there is a big demand for them by models and strippers who have to shave off their pubes for work but get a thrill from wearing little wigs on their Gates of Paradise whenever they go out.

'I'll have one of them', said my mate, rising to the occasion.

'What colour?' asked the retail executive.

'Well, that blonde one really turns me on', said Seamus.

'I suppose you want me to gift-wrap it as well', laughed the sales operative.

'No way', said my mate. 'I'll eat it here thank you.'

Funnily enough, the subject of Tasmania also reminds me of this interesting little story:

A bloke gets stranded on a desert island off Tazzie. The only other inhabitants of the island are a big dog and a pig. After a few weeks the poor bastard starts feeling a bit randy and, believe it or not readers, he starts fancying the pig! The trouble is, every time he tries to get near his porky passion the bloody dog starts growling. This goes on for four months until, one day, a big piece of driftwood floats to shore carrying a gorgeous young blonde sheilah, *absolutely bollock naked*.

The girl walks up to the bloke, who's grinning from ear to ear. 'Christ am I glad to see you', he says.

'I'm glad to see you too', says the sheilah in a sexy voice. 'Is there anything I can do for you?'

'You bet there is', says the bloke, 'You can take that bloody dog for a walk'.

This is one of those jokes that are, sadly, all too rare these days. I'm talking about the sort of joke you can tell in front of the wife and nippers or at a garden party at Buck House - *no worries*.

BANGKOK and MANILA

I've always liked the name Bangkok because that's exactly
what most of the women there do. As for Manila, it's such a
raunchy little stopover that if you step off the plane and
take a deep breath you could almost cop a dose. The
Philippino conurbation has also given its name to the buff
envelope so dear to Civil Servants the world over. Why
waste your time in Hong Kong with these two delightful
oriental metropoli only a few drinks away on a VIP jet at
the Australian Taxpayer's expense?

Would you believe the Lady Patterson once accompanied me on a government mission to Bangers back in the
rock'n'rolling 60's? While she got stuck into the Thai silk, I
got stuck into the Thai velvet. In them days the name
Patterson was pretty well synonymous with Australian
culture and I was working on my novel *Between Thai
Thighs*, a no-holes-barred scathing indictment of the
Vietnam War told in terms of a horny little Australian
Hippie who gets sucked into the white slave markets
of Malaysia. A mate of mine on the Yartz Council swung
me a five-figure, tax-free, non-refundable grant to write
this confrontative and controversial publication and to
their shame, world publishers were just too shit-scared to
print it.

Whenever I go to Bangkok I'm always as busy as a
one-armed taxi driver with crabs and by now my readers
will have gathered I'm a bit of a maverick in the political
spectrum because I am that rare species who can cop a joke
at his own expense. Here is a beauty in respect of and
relating to a recent trip. Frankly, I was as full as a seaside
shithouse on Boxing Day after a pretty gruelling conference on world hunger and I was cruising around Bangers in
my air-conditioned government limmo af four o'clock in
the morning with a view to unwinding in some congenial
rub-and-tug shop. A mate of mine from Sydney – let's call
him Mr Justice O'Shaughnessy – had given me a good

address on the back of a matchbox but somehow or other I ended up in a bloody Chiropodist's surgery instead. I don't know if I have mentioned it but I'd had a couple that night, so I didn't *know* I was in a Chiropodist's. All I did was stand in a quaint little oriental cubicle and haul out the old one-eyed trouser snake, but as soon as the little doll-faced Thai sheilah came around the corner and saw what I was up to she squealed out:

'That's not a foot!'

'I know it isn't darling', I replied quick as a flash, 'but it's near enough so get cracking on it'.

Not bad for four am with a skinful is it? And I've told that one against myself on many occasions with great success except once when it went down like a lead boomerang at a YWCA lunch for disabled Aboriginal parents without partners.

THE GULF

I've just been up the Gulf and, although that sounds promising, I'm here to tell you that those old teatowel-heads know how to make it uphill work for a hard-nosed trouble-shooter like me, who works hard and given half the chance, likes to play hard too. Mature students and Open University types probably know which of the old Pharoahs used to rave on about 'A bit of cheese, a glass of wine and Thou', but whoever it was – probably the fuckin' Sphinx himself – a jug of wine in Saudiland is about as hard to find as nookie in a nunnery.

For my sins I arranged a bit of a cheese conference in that part of the world recently, in honour of the aforementioned poem (let's face it, probably the most famous cheese poem in history for Christ's sake) and I got nothing but aggro from a bunch of thirst-crazed delegates. Some of the hotels turn on the grog for the benefit of expatriates who don't like eating on an empty stomach, but the teatowel-heads really charge like a wounded bull for liquid necessities, and not all western visitors have the slush fund which I have the good fortune to carry thanks to the generous offices of the A.T.P.*

In some places around the Gulf they can chop off your hand for galloping the lizard, though paradoxically I've never seen so many shepherds standing around in the hotel lobbies scratching their balls. Still, I guess if you had to heave a camel onto the back seat of an air-conditioned, stretch-bodied Mercedes every morning, you'd stand a chance of picking up a bit of livestock in the short and curlies!

The womenfolk have obviously spent a bit of time in Knightsbridge Street and Harley Road, London, because they've copied the Belgravian idea of wearing those leather masks and in my book the old Middle East custom of veiling the sheilahs has got a lot going for it. Many's the

* Australian Tax Payer

time in the early hours of the morning I've thought how much better Gwennie's head would look up a Yashmak.

The Sheiks go in for bigamy in a big way and none of the sheilahs seem to mind the set-up, so long as they've got a Harrods charge card, a colour TV in the back of the limmo and a new set of gold choppers from some Harley Road fang-bandit. Some of the dentists who have really cleaned up fitting the teatowel-heads with new sets of top-of-the-range, state-of-the-art gob crockery turn out to be – you've guessed it – Aussies, and you'd be surprised how many cavities they can find when the customer's asleep in the chair.

A mate of mine usually X-rays their wallets before he even takes an optic in their mouths. Incidentally, another popular operation favoured by the female members of the dish-cloth and fan-belt brigade has kept a few gynos from Down Under in Porsches and Lear Jets for yonks. I refer to the little nip and tuck which turns a sheilah who's copped a length back into a virgin. Incidentally, have you heard my definition of a gyno? A spreader of old wives' tails! Although some of those old desert rams like to put it about, they are not interested in buying damaged goods when it comes to the womenfolk.

A lot of hosties have a pretty good time when they are laid over in this part of the world. Should a sheikh's beady eye fall upon them, then it's Easy Street, Fat City and a good deal better than shoving a grog trolley up the aisle of a Boeing past a lot of boozed-up Samsonite-bashers from Birmingham. But not all these sheilahs who opt for Harem happiness get lucky, and the old fashioned expression 'What's in it for me?'; '*Sand*', certainly applies to the occasional little stewardess who has rashly settled for a bottom-of-the-range Cartier watch and a Bedouin bazooka up her back bottie.

Some of those oil billionaires don't like it plain and simple and a few of their little blonde protégées have often painfully wondered why a land so rich in oil is so short of petroleum jelly.

14

How to Handle the Media

Currently, I've had a long and politically improbable friendship with the Rupert Murdochs of this world because, as Australia's number one Ambassador, carpet-bagging troubleshooter and hard nosed, pragfuckinmatic maverick from way back, I'm in the business of being a Survivor *per se*, across the board. *Are you with me?*

At the end of the day, from where I sit, this means I've got a responsibility in terms of the world media to put Australia's message across. The old image of a yobbo in a dirty singlet, a chilled tube in his hand and corks hanging off his hat is about as accurate as saying that the average Brit wears a monocle, bowler hat, furled umbrella and *works!* The aforementioned dirty libel on Australia's image is the result of a carefully orchestrated shit-slinging campaign by a few élitist ex-pats, traitors and plummy-voiced kapok-krunchers who make a quid in the colour supplements of Europe bucketing their bushland heritage. In my book this type is lower than the basic wage. He's that low, in fact, that he could parachute out of a snake's arsehole and *still free-fall!*

In spite of the well known statistic that Australia has got more culture per square inch than a month-old mango, there's a type of ex-pat Australian journo who gets off on shafting his old mates back home, and, frankly, I wouldn't piss in his ear if his brain was on fire. Needless to say I've got to chuck the old Press Conference wherever I go to set the record straight and I'm here to tell you I'm winning, *no worries*. This very publication you are perusing, financed in part by the Sydney Sophistication Switchboard (literature division), will be an eye-opener to a lot of people who put my country pretty low on the list of travel priorities, somewhere between Belfast and the Falkland Islands.

Press Conferences

Anyone can hold a Press Conference. Just remember to stick the word 'Refreshments' on the inivitation and you'll get more journos rolling up than you can poke a stick at. Currently, the World Press tend to associate my name with fillums, cheese, wheelchair-compatible Opera Houses and the Yartz in general. If I'm wearing my cheese hat and we're announcing a new breakthrough in Tasmanian Gorgonzola for instance, then I organise a few nice little Antipodean horn-bags who don't mind flashing their norks in public and haven't got too many bruises on their bums, to mingle with the guests in clean G-strings, carrying trays of cholesterol-enriched Oz dairy produce.

There's nothing like a near-naked sheila with a decent set of zit-free fun-bags brushing the Brie, and the unmistakeable odour of over-ripe Canberra Camembert, to get those tired old tucker correspondents interested in what the Australian cheese producer is currently sticking up the international market. Funnily enough, I was currently sitting on the Cheese Board this morning and that can be uncomfortable – those little flags get up your arse! Seriously though, I've dreamed up some great slogans emphasizing aroma and staying power because, let's face it, our cheese products stay under your fingenails longer than most and I'm introducing thc World Press to the Australian Sniff Test next month at the Cheddar Gorge Cheese Fair with slogans like: 'Which finger has been up the Ayers Roquefort?' *Sniff it and see.*

The essence of these promotions is to have plenty of nubile she-meat moving around and a pretty well constant supply of local lager. The name of the game is credibility and that means a nice, striped seersucker suit and for Christ's sake don't say that with a mouthful of Brie, beer and buttered bikkies.

Getting the jump on the Press

Then there's the one-to-one Press Conference in your office. If it's a lady journo then it's a breeze, no worries. Just make sure they send you a young spunk and not some old lezzo with a face like a poultice hanging over a hospital balcony. Make sure you're standing behind her when she bends over to take the portable tape recorder out of her bag. A glimpse of the odd hygiene item tucked away amongst her keys and face powder is your cue to suggest the interview might be usefully continued over a long lunch. And always ensure that you see female reporters late in the morning since chances are you'll be giving them more than an interview in a motel suite while they're still washing down the Black Forest Gâteau with their fourth Irish Coffee.

On one occasion I was in such a hurry to give a lass a really in-depth interview after lunch that she was still chewing while I was climbing back into my strides. It's not a bad idea to have an adult video going when a trainee journette nervously creeps into your office. Just tell her you're checking out a bit of raunchy footage with a view to banning it in Australian geriatric facilities. With any luck it'll turn her on and she might even forget why she came, or how many times for that matter.

Fleet Street is stacked with mates of mine and I've never had a bad press but you've still got to watch the odd Australian male journo with a chip on his shoulder the size of the Opera House who brown-noses his way into your office. If you've made it overseas to the extent that I have for Christ's sake, you'll always find some little turd with a typewriter ready to do a hatchet job on you – but bet your life he's got half a socially relevant novel in the bottom drawer of his desk so you've only got to hint that you're on the lookout for a good family fillum script about Ronald Reagan's role in the massacre of Tasmanian Abbos to get the bastard grovelling.

Chat Shows

Whenever I hit town I keep a pretty high profile, *no worries*, and the best way to maintain it is to get the old Patterson head on the box. I've been chatted up by the best of them too, from Michael Parkinson to Clive James. Parky's got the old chat show game by the balls and he knows every wrinkle in the business just as we've got to know every wrinkle on old Parky's chops. He's got a mouth on him like the wrong end of a plucked fowl and he wouldn't last ten seconds in my wife's kitchen at Christmas because she'd be up his gob with a handful of sage and onions. But he's a nice little bugger and he reckons me, Henry Kissinger and Mother Teresa are his star interviewees.

My compatriot Clive James has also engaged me in the odd meaningful dialogue but remember when you're on his show that old Clive fancies his chances as a comic, so get ready to piss yourself laughing. Just don't wave your hands about too much or you'll block the autocue upon which old Clive's eyeballs are permanently fixed. The producer won't thank you for making them glaze over with panic.

The wireless is pretty much a thing of the past for top-level communicators like me, but enough to say I recently gave a talk on Disabled Australian Puppet Theatre for Parents Without Partners which was networked coast to coast in Iceland. In fact the eskimos and blubber-bashers were igloo'd to their sets. *With me?*

Incidentally – and this is in Club – a few old mates of mine and upper echelon high-flyers in the Australian Public Service who are still doing the right thing on Sunday mornings, are trying to wangle me a Papal Audience. I know that fantastic old Polish tarmac-basher is creaming his cassock for a nice long chin-wag with Yours Truly in the privacy of his own Basilica and I reckon on that occasion I'll have to cut Gwennie into the action. The Old Minister of War is still practising and I must say if there was a photo of her on the front page of the *Sydney Herald* with a black doily on her head, chewing the fat with His Holiness, the next door neighbours would really reckon Gwen's shit didn't stink. I guess this tells you I love the old battleaxe, and that's an *exclusive!*

15

Grooming for the Man on the Move

I'm a seasoned traveller. In other words after a long trip wrestling with the in-flight condiments, trying to rip open the sauce sachets while sipping Bloody Marys in the middle of turbulence, I generally emerge the other end well seasoned from head to foot. Travel plays merry hell with a decent suit and many is the brand new seersucker job I've left home in which was rooted twenty-four hours later.

Fortunately in most of the cities where I do business there's a one-hour dry cleaning service just around the corner from my preferred rub-and-tug shop, so while I'm getting over the jet-lag on a waterbed with a couple of Malaysian physios and a bottle of baby oil, the receptionist is whipping my strides, or whatever other garment has succumbed to the hazards of travel, around to the nearest valet service.

In spite of my radical political stance *vis-à-vis* across the board I'm a bit of a conservative old bastard in terms of some respects and whenever I nip into a Pharmacy to pick up the odd precaution, I prefer to do business with a bloke. 'I'd like to speak to the chemist please', is what I usually say when a horny little sheilah with a short white coat, a love bite and pair of Dr Scholls rushes to serve me. I guess I've got too much respect for women to risk embarrassing them in front of their peer group and all that shampoo and shit paper, to ask them to sell me across the counter what under other circumstances with the lights off and a skinful of Harvey Wallbangers, they would happily tie knots in and chuck under the bed.

Likewise, when the girl at the dry cleaner's asks me to identify a particularly tenacious and somewhat crusty stain, I generally ask to speak to the Dry Cleaner himself and then I sometimes write it down on a bit of paper, spinning some yarn about a mate of mine who borrowed the suit for his stag night and honeymoon. I wouldn't want to unduly upset an innocent little laundress, though I have to laugh sometimes to think what Lady Patterson, my number one Gofer, has washed out of my undergarments with her red old hands without smelling a rat, the Lord love her.

The wise jet-setter slips into a floppy old track-suit when faced with a long haul. For one thing it doesn't matter what you spill down it and for another you don't have to get undressed in those cramped little airborne dunnies to choke a darkie or give some hostie a quick knee-trembler. I'll never forget when I once gave one to a randy little stewardess. I was thirty thousand feet and eight inches up at the time and just as I was getting into the vinegar strokes, someone started hammering on the door. It turned out to be a pillow-biting steward asking me if I was alright. Apparently my bum kept hitting the emergency button on the toilet wall!

Keeping my end up

But my problem as a front man for Australia is that I've got to keep up appearances. What would the world at large think of my homeland if its best known roving Ambassador dressed like a hippie. That's why I'm a suit man and it's not for nothing I've logged umpteen nominations for Best Dressed Man in Australia. The Lord gave us our bodies and, for all I know, he gave me mine as well and it behoves us to look after them. You get your car serviced don't you? And on the same principle I get my anatomy serviced even more regularly. My old mate the A.T.P. has pumped big bikkies into Les Pattersson and I have a keen sense of responsibility to the men, women and children I serve. I'm a *role model* for Christ's sake!

Our family quack looks me over once in a blue moon and gives me an A1 bill of health too, no worries. The bastard ought to because I pulled a few strings and got him planning permission for an extension to his beach house and it only cost him a case of Scotch and a grand's worth of readies in a brown paper envelope.

Dr Fennessy has always had a bee in his bonnet about my liver being slightly over-sized. 'What's new Doc?' is what I say because he'd only have to drop his stethoscope down my strides to discover that I go in for enlarged organs in a big way. In fact when I'm with a girl for the first time, I generally tell her to put the head in and walk slowly towards me. The Doc is pretty broad-minded too, so after a particularly arduous fact-finding mission in places like Manila and Haiti, I nip into his office for the odd blood test just in case the CIA bastards or the enemies of Australian Socialism have set me up with a shonky sheilah and I've copped more clap than a Joanie Sutherland ballet. I don't want to come the blue-nosed wowser but I reckon every loving husband and devoted family man owes it to his nearest and dearest to slap his walloper on the pox doctor's desk at least one a month.

A colleague of mine once went to the quack because he thought he'd copped a dose and the Doc asked him if his old fella burned after he'd had a naughty.

'No Doc,' he replied, 'I've never thought of lighting it'.

Every now and then you strike a senior member of the Australian Public Service who's obviously slipped past the wicket keeper.

How Green Was My Valium

I always like to call in to see old Des as I've come to call Doc Fennessy. He enjoys a sip himself, the old hypocrite, and he gives me the latest low-down on Gwen, the Lady

Patterson. 'Depression' was her medical problem at the last count, whatever that might mean. I guess if the womenfolk have got nothing wrong with them they've got to make something up. Des reckoned she'd told him she had a Valium problem so he'd asked her how many more she needed. He said the wives of most top executives turned into raving ratbags sooner or later in spite of the fact they had colour TV, Volvos and a fridge full of Sherry. Generally, after he'd bunged them on Valium for life, they were as good as gold and since most of them were hooked on sad shows like *Dynasty* and *Dallas*, nobody thought it was a bit surprising to see them sitting at home howling their eyes out round the clock.

Des told me a funny story that he'd kept under wraps for yonks. He reckoned that Gwen had come to see him after our honeymoon with a few leading questions.

'What's that long thing between Les's legs?' she asked innocently.

'That's his penis,' replied the doc.

'And what is that thing on the end?'

'That's the head or glans.'

'Oh, and what are the two things about eleven inches behind the head?'

'Well Mrs Patterson, I don't know about your husband, but on me they'd be the cheeks of my arse.'

Des Fennessy told me he still pissed himself at that and he'd been bottling it up for years.

TRAVEL STAINS

There's an old Aboriginal expression, the Lord be good to them, which roughly translated means: there's many a slip twixt the grub and the lip. This is a reference to witchetty grubs which, like all ethnic delicacies, would more than likely have you and mc going for the big spit and yodelling into the white telephone. Likewise there's many a slip between the drink and the vip (as in V.I.P.) and I've got hand-stitched seersucker to prove it.

I don't know what it is about me, but as soon as women see me they want to take me to the cleaners. I guess it's my high-pressure, knock-about, freewheeling, trouble-shooter's life-style that leaves an indelible impression on them and, from time to time, on my high-fashion, Australian-fibre leisure wear.

Here are a few simple old antidotes which have helped keep me squeaky clean in spite of the fact that I move faster than a tin of worms with an outboard motor.

Beer
Sponge with water to which a little ammonia has been added, or rinse in warm vinegar water. If all else fails, telex Hong Kong for another suit and charge it to the A.T.P.

Blood
If wet, soak in cold water first, then add a few drops of household ammonia to the water. If dry blood, soak in a solution of 1 dessertspoon salt to 3 cups water. And don't forget to ask the sheilah for a refund.

Chocolate
First soak fabric in cold water containing detergent. Don't use hot water, it sets the stain. For fast cottons (if stain is still there), use bleach; for woollens, borax. A lot of hotels booked for me by the Australian Government are the up-market variety which provide little touches like a couple of chocolates on the pillow. I vividly recall a research assistant of mine seeing this for the first time and saying coyly: 'Can I eat it now?' to which I replied, 'be my guest and if you do it right I'll give you a chocolate'.

Chunder
If dry, scrape off with spatula or chip off with a palate knife. Soak in tepid water with a pinch of borax and detergent. Whizz off to the dry cleaner with some yarn about your wife's morning sickness, though if they're smart they will

wonder how she managed to hit the back of your trousers where they may be deeply ingrained stains not inconsistent with a man in a hurry measuring his length on a dunny floor.

Chunder Vindaloo
Burn the suit.

Sperm
Dissolve a teaspoon of salt in 1½ cups of warm water and sponge stain. Repeat with clear water. (Do not use hot water or the albumen will coagulate. You know what happens in the bath fellas.)

16

Where I'm Coming From

Readers of this publication will have gathered by now that I'm a man who does his homework. Boy oh boy, does that word 'homework' take me back to Australia's prestige 'Our Lady of Dolours' boys' school where I first learnt to marticulate. I remember once being given a composition to write called 'What I did in the holidays' and did that get me six of the best on the bare bum from Father Rafferty! I guess honesty was always my number one problem. It's certainly a problem I try not to inflict on the wife more than I can help it, the Lord bless her. By cripes though, education has come a long way since the old days when me and my peer group used to play knuckle-bones and hoppo-bumpo in the dust under the peppercorns.

My young Craig has got quite a head on his shoulders according to his headmaster who has just bunged an extension on his beach house since I swung him the planning permission. Craig's report cards have certainly taken a turn for the better lately and that young bloke of mine is currently getting stuck into computer games like Space Invaders which really puts his grey matter to the test. Karen is more of a book-worm and currently last week she wrote an essay on the evils of apartheid. Her teacher, Ross Pappadopolos reckons she might just have written the most scathing indictment of white atrocities in South Africa yet penned by an Australian school kid who has never been farther than Bondi.

My Karen is her father's daughter and she's developing quite a social conscience. With her aerosol spray she's certainly teaching the neighbours how to spell Nicaragua. Those kids are as proud as buggery of me and they've got photos of me with world famous personalities all over their bulletin boards.

I was home the weekend before last and I got my driver to run Karen to her speech therapist, wait for her and take her on to Weight Watchers. Jerry (that's my driver, and he's aptly named – he's always full. I once said, 'Jerry you're that full, your place is under the bed.') reckoned Karen was like Lady Muck in the back seat of the Commonwealth limmo, stopping every few minutes so she could whip out the aerosol and hit someone's fence with a bit of anti-nuke graffiti. Currently, the Pope's a Jew if that daughter of mine isn't a cert for the political spectrum one day.

I go deep

My Gwen is knocking herself out trying to matriculate at the Open Uni of Sydney these days so on those few occasions when we coincide, she tends to come on a bit strong with the Philosophy. I let her rip.

I never go into anything too deeply with a woman, INTELLECTUALLY speaking that is, and I haven't been into anything with Gwen for yonks.

What pisses me off, if you'll excuse the slightly crude expression, is that, as a result, my wife is actually beginning to have her doubts about whether or not there's ever been a Superior Being up there. Now I'm no bloody saint for Christ's sake, but I yield to none in my abhorrence of elitist Uni-types bucketing the Good Book. Are you with me?

As a matter of fact, there was a time in my early life when I very nearly donned the cassock, and if I had, my old mum would have swung with joy on her rosary from the highest gum tree. Mum always hoped I might become the first

Australian Pope and this is the only time (sober) I've ever let that one out. I guess a few Dago grease-ball bastards at the Vatican are the only people who ever knew how close they were to shifting the Holy See to Sydney Harbour.

But I reached a spiritual crossroads where I had to choose between Church (and a possible job at the top involving celibacy) and the service of my beloved Homeland (with as much horizontal endeavour as an ATP-funded Gold Amex card can buy). The fact that I failed Latin at Our Lady of Dolours played a small part in the decision as well. Mind you, these days I spend a lot of time on my knees, but not in church. In fact, come to think of it, it's a year or two since I sniffed the old incense. Nevertheless, strong religious beliefs are among the many things I still hold firmly to my bosom. No Uni ratbag can try and tell me the good Lord didn't throw this ripper planet together, although after deep theological discussions with my Girl Friday, Brigit, I find myself coming around to the Big Bang Theory. *Are you with me?*

Currently, I believe confession is good for the soul (so long as the wife doesn't find out the details) but my routine Diary of Dirty Deeds got a bit on the repetitive side over the years, so I knocked off a tape recording of my standard sins. Eventually, due to pressures of Affairs of State, I kicked the habit of going to confession personally, sending Jerry, my devout driver, who would sneak into the cubicle, whip out his Hitachi, and say, 'Bless him Father, for Sir Les has sinned', then he'd hit the button and smoke a few fags while the cassette rolled.

I had to pack this in though when that hungry bastard Jerry stuck it up me for time-and-a-half for doing *my* penance for Christ's sake. *And it wasn't even Sunday!*

Splashing out

I yield to none in my abhorrence of chauvinism. I love women and women love me. I can't get enough of them, though I bet they sometimes wish they could accommodate a little less of me. But I don't give my all to the womenfolk, and if you don't believe me ask Geoff Bolton, the manager of my local sperm bank to take you on a guided tour of the vaults and show you the Patterson Vat. Geoff reckons it's incredible the number of childless couples who specifically request a red-hot burst of L.P. Sauce.

I've got to know the Sister down there (Cheryl Hocking) pretty well, and I've never seen a sheilah before who's been jealous of a test tube. She reckons I'm her easiest client, and she never has to lend a helping hand. All she does is put the kettle on for a cup of tea, chuck the latest *Penthouse* over the top of the screen, and it's all over before her whistle starts to blow. It's funny to think there are little cots sprinkled around the planet containing nippers with the famous Patterson profile. Cheryl reckons I'm fantastic the way I think of that bank wherever my diplomatic duties take me. In fact, I'm the only customer who makes airmail deposits from as far away as Hamburg and Bangkok. She says it's a pleasure opening the envelope with her teeth, but it's a bastard having to tackle a rubber reef knot. This is just one of many examples of the Les Patterson Philosophy on Giving. I was born with plenty, and I like to spread it around, no worries.

Back at the wife-cage

Whenever I come home the old Minister of War pretends to play it cool as though I've just been down the street for a few minutes to buy a packet of smokes. Even if I've been away for six weeks she sticks out her cheek for a peck and I can see she's still got her eyes glued to 'The Young Doctors'. She was always a wowser about the booze but after all these years she's beginning to see the light, judging by the odd voddy miniature I've discovered behind our wedding photo in the lounge. I'm keenly observant and I can always tell she's been chucking make-up at her face seconds before I came in the door by the powder clinging

to her shoulders and the patches she missed with the
electrolysis needle. Bless her heart, she really makes an
effort for the first few minutes – and doesn't even scratch
her eczema.

There was a photo of her once in the *Canberra Times*
where she could have been mistaken for a beauty queen
and funnily enough that's just what happened. There was
a picture of Miss Australia, a sheilah called Mary Anne
Kosnjak, with Gwen's name underneath by mistake. I guess
when they got the photo of Gwen the Union threatened
industrial action if they were forced to print it. You might
think I'm being a bit tough on Gwen but there's nothing on
this page I wouldn't say to her face to face. That's the kind
of relationship we've got and it's beautiful.

I've promised my Gwen a wonderful trip to Los Angeles
for her next birthday because I know for a cert I'm going to
be in Paris at the time and also because I've booked her in
with one of the top cosmetic surgeons in the business.
Currently, he works out of Forest Lawn Cemetery and
Gwen will be the first living client he's tackled, but he
assured me that any mistakes would be knocked off the bill.
A couple of Gwen's mates, wives of Australian High Court
Judges and Senior Cabinet Ministers, have had a bit of
'landscaping' and the odd nip and tuck and not only does
Gwennie want to get in on the act but she's sick of wearing
that bag over her head at dinner parties at my request. I'm
only kidding readers. She takes it *off* for dinner and *she's
the best kid in the world*.

17

The Australian Tongue

How and Where to use it

I yield to none in my abhorrence of bad language, and there's nothing worse in my book than a sheilah with a dirty mouth. My wife Gwen, let's face it, has been through the mill – health-wise she's been up and down like a toilet seat all her life – and if ever a woman has been tempted to indulge in the occasional profanity, she has. But Lady Patterson would have to be the exception. These days, I regret to say, sheilahs are a foul-mouthed mob, and some of the things Girl Fridays have said to me in the heat of the moment would make your hair curl. In point of fact, they *will* make your hair curl too because I'm about to tell you what some of these appalling expressions are.

A French sheilah who works for UNESCO nearly screamed the place down one night and if her interpreter, a Mademoiselle Zou Zou, hadn't been in the cot with us at the time, I would have been spared the embarrassment of knowing what she wanted. Unfortunately, I can't tell you exactly what it was because I can't remember the French for *Kiss me where it smells*. Sorry readers, but for bedroom talk, that's over the top in anyone's lingo.

Believe it or not, a really nice, upper class Pom tart called Camilla (aren't they all?), once said to me in the middle of a mega-buck lunch at the Ritz Hotel, 'If you think I'm going to drop my dainties for a crude colonial like you, you've got another thing coming'. I don't know about you readers, but

I believe this kind of talk only degrades Womanhood, even when it comes from the lips of a sheila who is obviously a raving lezzo.

Because I have access to classified information, you can bet your life the KGB have been trying to crack me for years. Once a little sheila from the typing pool of the Russian Consulate in West Berlin offered me a nibble of her furburger in her well furnished second floor apartment. Just when I was beginning to wish I could breathe through my ears, I heard the unmistakable click of a Box Brownie, and I realised I was being sexually exploited by an unscrupulous, if not unattractive, ideological ratbag. After I threw her off the bed and shoved the film up her darkroom, I heard language from that young woman's lips that would have made a veteran kangaroo-crutcher blush. My problem is I put sheilahs on a pedestal, but let's face it, tell me a better way to take an optic of a percy-purse, *are you with me?*

I'm pretty good on my feet as the occasional air hostess has had cause to remark when standing up has been the only option. I was born with the gift of the gab and though we Aussies don't like to trace our lineage back too far, I reckon if you shook the old Patterson family tree a few silver-tongued Irishmen could well drop out. The mouth is Australia's number one orifice and, being an optimist, I always keep mine ajar.

In my job I have to do a lot of public speaking and I never need notes. It's all off the top of my head, like this book. If I've got a refreshing glass of neck-oil in one hand, a smoke on the go in the other and the hand of a good woman tucked between my knees, I can keep a table-full of diplomats, foreign dignitaries and media free-loaders spellbound for minutes flat. Don't ask me how I do it because more often than not I've just stepped off a plane with no time to hit the fart-sack and barely enough for a quick AP&C* job in my VIP suite and a squirt of duty free.

* Armpit and crutch.

There's a few people in Australia who call themselves socialites but I doubt if anyone from England or even the States, where they're as rough as guts, would take that claim seriously if they met them. They are generally well-heeled Proddies who never had a convict in the family, though if I could trace the descendants of the Pommie judge who sent old Ebenezer Patterson to Australia in the Middle Ages, I'd shake the bastard by the hand because that old beak made it possible, without knowing it, for me to be born in the greatest little country in the world.

Currently, I usually relate that anecdote when I make a speech, whether it be in public or in private. It can be used while launching a big-budget Australian fillum, opening a wheelchair-compatible Aboriginal reserve, accepting the Americas Cup, kicking off a cheese campaign, consoling an AIDS victim, chatting to an Australian dole-clerk or categorically denying scurrilous, tasteless, baseless and carefully-orchestrated allegations of government corruption at the highest level.

Whenever I talk in public I get laughs, particularly in the States and Pommieland where they seem to think the Australian turn of phrase is funny. Although I'm currently an International Statesman, I suppose if you listen to me very carefully you could still pick up the fact that I was born in Sydney and I'm not ashamed of it. There are a few words and phrases which occasionally slip through the wicket keeper when I'm waxing rhetorical and the odd one could suffer in translation so if you're planning a trip Down Under, you could do worse than bone up on a few standard expessions unique to my island continent.

Naturally there are cultural differences and time-honoured customs which even the most adaptable Yank or Brit will never surmount. A couple of years ago I had the onerous job of showing some chinless wonder from England over the Australian outback. After a couple of weeks he started getting randy and the silly prick took a fancy to an old ethnic minority sheilah who lived in a hut in the back paddock. After holding off for a month, he sneaked down there one night and while he was knocking her off, one of her mangy dogs came sniffing around the bed.

'Piss off', she yelled, 'You had your turn this morning.'

The Pom leaped up horrified.

'Oh how ghastly – riding after hounds without a red coat.'

But just like the Frogs who change their tune from being arrogant dickheads as soon as you say *Bonjour*, the Australian even warms to a Pom if he makes a pathetic effort to speak the local lingo.

Les's Large Appendage

A Glossary of the Australian Language

Abbos (Abos) *dimin. pl. n.* Boomerang chuckers; a great little bunch of blokes.

aboriginal activist *n.* A Yugo ratbag and media freak whose great-great-uncle once stunned a numbat with a boomerang.

Adrian *adj.* Inebriated; rhyming slang for Adrian Quist [1913–   ], famed Australian tennis player.

amber fluid *n.* Australia's preferred lubricant.

approachable *adj.* A politician or law enforcement officer susceptible to discreet financial inducement.

apricots *phr.* **up to the apricots** Most of my secretaries know my position on this one; an infallible yardstick for measuring human affection.

arrogant dickhead *phr.* A charismatic politician *after* he's been elected Prime Minister (See **charisma**).

arvo *dimin. n.* Afternoon; Pommie luncheon period.

ATP *n.* The Australian taxpayer.

ball breaker *n.* A sheila who gives you the knock-back; a uni student.

barker's egg *n.* Dog turd (popular on British pavements).

bearded clams *pl. n.* Tasty morsels of tasty mortals.

Bermudas *phr.* **a case of the Bermuda shorts** Impecunious, short [rhyming slang].

big white telephone *n.* Dunny.

billabong *n.* Stagnant swamp [Abo.].

blue *phr.* **to have a blue** An altercation involving forceful language.

blurter *n.* Freckle.

body line *phr.* A carefully orchestrated attack on Australian cricket by a bunch of monocled Pommy Pooftahs.

bonzer *adj.* Stunning [arch.].

brown paper bag/envelope *n.* Australian politicians' and law enforcement officers' preferred receptacle for a backhander of readies.

brownie *n.* Blurter.

bucket *v.* To denigrate or bad-mouth.

bum's rush *n.* The shove.

bundle *phr.* **to drop one's bundle** To break wind [See under **lunch box**].

bush-buzzer *n.* The wife's best friend.

charisma *n.* (aboriginal?) An elusive quality possessed by Australian politicians *before* they are elected Prime Minister (See **arrogant dickhead**).

chockers *adj.* Full as a bull's bum/Catholic school/footie final/fairy's phone book, etc. [short for chock-a-block; perhaps Indian or Pakistani].

chocko *n.* A swarthy Grecian or Italian person.

choke a darkie *v.* To meditate on the big white telephone.

chuck *v. & n.* Chunder of a colourful and rich consistency.

chunder *v. & n.* See under **chuck**.

cobber *n.* A political colleague worth looking after [See under **brown paper bag**].

conchie *dimin. n.* A stupid brown-noser [short for conscientious].

crash-hot *adj.* Shit-hot [origin unknown].

Daphne *obs. n.* An uncalled-for type of Australian sheilah named after a long-forgotten lezzo.

date-packer *n.* A South Australian arts administrator.

donger *n.* A challenge to a decent tailor.

doughnut *n*. A non-fattening meal.

drongo *n*. See **droob**.

droob *n*. A cross between a drongo, a dill, a dag, a wet and a wimp.

dunny *n*. Powder-room [Abo.].

fat, to crack a *phr*. To think with one's body.

ferret *n*. My macho mascot. See **doughnut**.

flags out *phr*. **To have the flags out** [See **red sails**].

freckle *n*. See **blurter**.

Frenchies *n. pl*. Water-proof sleeping-bags for mice.

full *adj*. Replete with liquid refreshment, e.g., as full as a footie final, Pommie complaint box, etc.

fun bags *pl. n*. Norks.

furry hoop *n*. A doughnut [origin unknown].

goer *n*. A well-balanced female who knows on what side her bread is buttered.

hair pie *n*. A snorkeller's lunch.

hard word *phr*. **to put the hard word on** To offer a woman her heart's desire.

hoppo-bumpo *n*. A schoolboy game I always won.

hornbag *n*. A raunchy, yet appealing, bit of she-meat.

hostie *n*. A goer.

jerkle *n*. A circle of schoolboys engaged in onanistic practices.

joes *phr*. **to give one the joes** To give one the heebie-jeebies.

journo *n*. A drunk; a failed novelist.

kangaroo *n*. A large rodent.

kapok-kruncher *n*. See under **date-packer**.

kick-back *n*. See under **plain wrappers**.

knee-trembler *n*. A stand-up naughty.

knock-back *n*. See under **ball-breaker**, **lezzo**, **uni student**, etc.

knock-shop *n*. An adult relaxation facility.

lamington *n*. An Australian delicacy [named after a prominent Queensland politico].

laughing gear *n*. The mouth.

lay down misère *n*. Term used in solo whist, a dead cert, a walk-up start.

lezzo *n*. A sheilah who won't come to the party.

lizard *phr*. **to gallop the lizard** To twang the wire.

lunch *phr*. **to drop one's lunch** To fart [vulgar].

lunch box *phr*. **to open one's lunch box** To fart [vulgar].

Mick *n*. A left-footer.

mini series *n*. An Australian fillum that doesn't know when to stop.

minister of war *n*. The spouse [The Lord bless her!].

moolah *n*. Government grants and/or government revenue [Abo.].

muff muncher *n*. A snorkeller [also **muff diver**].

Nips *coll. pl. n.* The bastards who won the last war as far as I'm concerned.

Noah *n*. A popular fish [rhyming slang **Noah's Ark** shark].

norks *pl. n.* Fun bags.

nut chokers *pl. n.* Briefs.

ocker *n*. One of the lost tribes of Australia.

oil slicks *pl. n.* Grecians [See also **Tennant Creeks**].

one-prick princess *s. n.* A spouse [See also **minister of war**].

orchestrated *adj*. A typically culture-conscious Australian word.

oxymoron *n*. An Irish welder.

pan-handler *n*. An Australian playwright.

pavlova *n*. A New Zealand pudding named after a dancing daphne of yesteryear.

la Perouse *n*. Booze [rhyming slang].

pile-driver *n*. A date-packer [vulgar].

pillow-biter *n*. A kapok-cruncher.

pink oboe *n*. A conversation stopper.

pollywaffle *n*. Ethnic chocolate-coated confectionery that women can only play with two hands [Abo. + vulg.].

pooftah *n*. A decent bloke who hasn't met the right sheila and never will [vulgar and obsolete].

quokka *n*. A Westralian rat [obsolete].

ratbag *n*. An Australian enthusiast.

red sails *pl. n*. An expensive discovery after a good dinner.

ripper *adj*. Excellent; no worries!

root *v*. To tenderly embrace without trousers.

rorty *adj*. Raunchy and naughty [me all over!].

rub and tug shop *n*. A facility for fitness freaks.

rubbidy *n*. An hotel [rhyming slang].

Samsonite basher *n*. A commercial traveller.

scallywag *n*. A criminal's description of himself.

scam *n*. An American expression which has found its true home in Australia.

shag *v*. To root.

sheila [sheilah] *n*. A hornbag [vulgar and obsolete].

shirtlifter *n*. Pooftah [bent rhyming slang].

shonky *adj*. Sub-standard or shit-house quality [old English].

shoot through *phr*. To scarper, vamoose.

slash *n*. A discharge of urine.

sling *phr*. **to sling a bribe/kickback** See under **State Premier**.

slopie *n*. An industrious slant-eyed ethnic minority.

spag *n*. Probably not a Vietnamese; an Italian? [affectionate].

squiz *n*. An optic.

strides *n*. Trousers.

stubble *n*. An Australian staple; a chubby beer bottle.

stunning *adj*. Bonzer [modern Aust.].

sugar bag *n*. A traditional Australian receptacle for emoluments, readies and kickbacks [obs.].

Tasmania *n.* Universally used to describe baseless allegations against innocent politicians [See **oxymoron**].

Tasmania, map of *n.* A triangular bushy zone subject to extreme temperature changes.

technicolour yawn *n.* A liquid laugh.

Tennant Creek *n.* A Macedonian [rhyming slang].

thank you *phr.* Unique Australian usage for 'please', e.g., I'd like another beer, thanks'.

thong *n.* An informal Australian item of Taiwanese footwear not always acceptable in revolving restaurants.

throttling pit *n.* A powder room [origin unknown].

tiger, to park a *phr.* To puke prodigiously.

toey *adj.* A goer [turf usage].

Tongue sandwich *n.* A kiss to build a dream on.

trouser dance *n.* A traditional post-imbibition, pre-coital courtship ritual frequently performed with the lights off and in the presence of an unconscious partner.

tucker *n.* Blotting paper.

turps *phr.* **to nudge the turps** To enjoy liquid refreshment.

twig *phr.* **to drop off the twig, to jump the twig** A typically sensitive Australian reference to the fragility of life.

ugly stick *n.* A magic wand which has been waved at many a spouse and at most Daphnes.

vinegar strokes (*medical*) The penultimate phase in sexual connection when the active partner experiences a facial rictus similar to that produced by drinking vinegar (information supplied by a doctor).

walloper *n.* A donger.

wick *phr.* **to dip the wick** To make a woman's dreams come true.

wife's best friend *n.* A walloper.

wowser *n.* A stupid bastard or teetotaller [supposed to be an acronym of W(e) O(nly) W(ant) S(ocial) E(vils) R(emedied)].

yabbie *n.* (Y)oung (A)ustralian (B)oring (B)usinessman.
yartz *n.* Culture Australian style.
yellow velvet *n.* An amenable Oriental.
yuckkie *n.* Y(oung) U(rban) C(atholic) K(apok)-K(runcher).
Yugo *n.* A delightful Yugoslavian resident of Australia.
yummie *n.* Y(oung) U(pwardly) M(asticating) M(arsupial), [Aboriginal word].

zipper sniffer *n.* A bloody nuisance.

ORGAN DONATION (OPTIONAL)

In the sad event that the owner of this book croak during in-flight movie, therapeutic session in rub-and-tug shop, wine tasting, cheese sniffing or even lawful matrimonial congress, it is the aforementioned owner's express wish that his organ be dispatched to the following consignee by registered post:

Lady
Mrs
Miss _____

Address _____

_____

_____

_____

Important Addresses for the Man on the Move

Wife

_____
_____
_____
_____
_____
_____

Parish Priest

_____
_____
_____
_____
_____
_____

Work

_____
_____
_____
_____
_____
_____

Pub

_____
_____
_____
_____
_____

Goers

_____
_____
_____
_____
_____
_____
_____
_____
_____
_____
_____
_____
_____
_____
_____
_____
_____
_____
_____
_____
_____
_____
_____
_____
_____
_____
_____
_____
_____
_____
_____
_____
_____

Dead-cert Lezzos and Ball-breakers

_____
_____
_____
_____
_____
_____
_____
_____
_____
_____
_____
_____
_____
_____
_____
_____
_____
_____
_____
_____
_____
_____
_____
_____
_____
_____
_____
_____
_____
_____
_____
_____
_____
_____
_____
_____
_____
_____

Rub-and-tug Shops

_____
_____
_____
_____
_____
_____
_____
_____
_____
_____
_____
_____
_____
_____
_____

Sperm Bank

_____
_____
_____
_____
_____
_____
_____
_____
_____
_____
_____
_____
_____
_____

Sympathetic Dry Cleaning Specialists

_____
_____
_____
_____
_____
_____
_____
_____
_____
_____
_____
_____
_____
_____
_____
_____
_____
_____
_____
_____
_____
_____
_____
_____
_____
_____
_____
_____
_____
_____
_____
_____
_____
_____
_____
_____

Male-staffed Chemists

_____ _____
_____
_____
_____
_____
_____
_____
_____
_____
_____
_____
_____
_____
_____
_____

Discreet Urologists

_____
_____
_____
_____
_____
_____
_____
_____
_____
_____
_____
_____
_____
_____
_____
_____

'Approachable' Magistrates and Law Enforcement Officers

_____
_____
_____
_____
_____
_____
_____
_____
_____
_____
_____
_____
_____
_____
_____
_____
_____
_____
_____
_____
_____
_____
_____
_____
_____
_____
_____
_____
_____
_____
_____
_____
_____
_____
_____
_____
_____
_____
_____